Recollections
of the
Early Settlers
of
Montgomery County Alabama

and their Families

By: W.G. Robertson

Southern Historical Press, Inc.
Greenville, South Carolina

This volume was reproduced
from a personal copy located in
the Publishers private library

Please direct all correspondence and book orders to:
SOUTHERN HISTORICAL PRESS, Inc.
PO Box 1267
Greenville, SC   29602-1267

Originally published 1892
Montgomery, Alabama
ISBN #978-1-63914-235-4
Printed in the United States of America

To My Old Friend,

GOV. THOMAS H. WATTS,

This Little Book is Respectfully

DEDICATED.

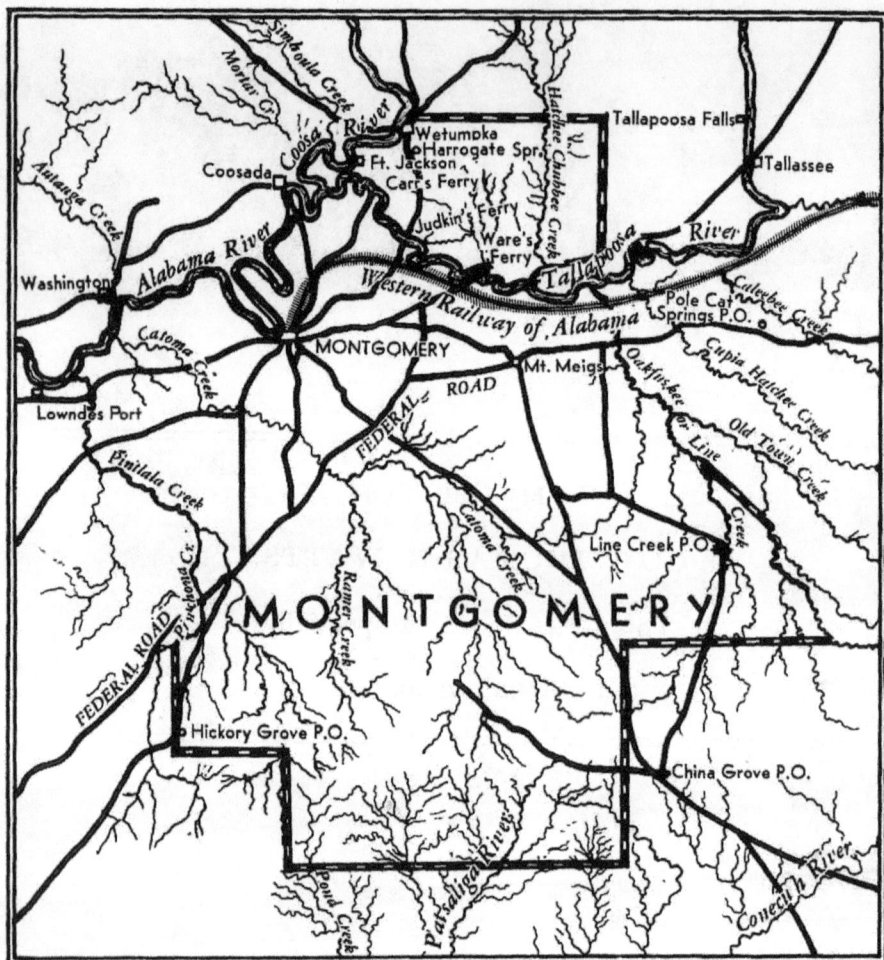

"In 1836 Henry LaTourette of Mobile compiled the first comprehensive map of the State of Alabama. This map portrays the face of our county as it appeared during the era covered by this book. The drawing which appears above was adapted from the LaTourette map especially for this reprinting of Robertson's "Recollections.""

PREFACE.

This little book has been written entirely from memory. In the year 1832, the writer, while a young man, assisted his father as Census Enumerater, and visited every family in the county; in order to get the proper enumeration, age and sex of every household. Again, from 1844 to 1848, he collected the tax for his father, and in 1848 was himself elected Tax Collector, and at the end of the term was elected Tax Assessor, and subsequently to that time he was more or less connected with the tax business in Montgomery county to the end of the war, therefore his opportunity was good for knowing these early settlers.

THE AUTHOR

MONTGOMERY COUNTY.

Before the State of Alabama was organized and admitted into the Federal Union it was known as the Mississippi Territory, and when Montgomery county was first surveyed and laid off it embraced what was known as the fork of the Coosa and Tallapoosa rivers, and remained a portion of the county up to about the beginning of the late war. It is now a portion of Elmore county. It also embraced the territory from a few miles east of Greenwood, then called High Log in Bullock county, to the Lowndes county line a distance of about forty miles east and west and from near Wetumpka to Briar Hill in Pike county, north and south, a distance of about forty-five miles. Montgomery county at that time was about forty miles square. The objection to the fork being a portion of Montgomery county, was the Tallapoosa river. In crossing the river to and from Montgomery, on horse-back or with buggies, wagons, etc., the ferriage would amount to as much annually to the people as their State and county tax. The objection to the eastern portion of the county was the distance the citizens had to travel to the court house; some of the citizens were compelled to travel a distance of thirty-five miles to reach the court house. At an early day there was an effort made to get the court house moved to a more central point, but on account of the Alabama river and steam boat facilities, the effort met with very little favor. The new counties of Elmore, Bullock and Crenshaw embrace a portion of the original survey of Montgomery county.

AUGUSTA.

At a very early day in the history of the county Montgomery had a rival, in a nice little town twelve miles above the city on the Tallapoosa river. It was located on a beautiful spot on the bank of the river, and had at one time between fifty and seventy-five family residences, with store-houses, hotels, academy, black-smith and wood shops, tailor shops, etc.; but after a few years the place proved to be sickly, and it was abandoned altogether. Augusta was the name of the town. Then everything centered to

MONTGOMERY,

the only town in the county, and a very small place. A man by the name of Andrew Dexter owned a tract of land near the business portion of the town, and he built a house for his goats to shelter in on the hill where the Capitol stands, and that hill was called Goat Hill until the first Capitol was built. Down below Goat Hill John Goldthwaite had a store, and the house was weatherboarded with white oak boards; and still further down, where the

Government building and post-office now stands, there was a little double pine-pole cabin, fenced in with pine rails and used as a tavern, the only one in town. And still further down, on what is now Dexter Avenue, to the old court house, situated where the basin now is, on both sides of the street stood little store houses, and before each door was a horse-rack for customers to hitch their horses. The firms of Mayhew & Whitman, and of Carpenter & Colclough, were among the merchants at that time. Whenever a farmer would bring in his few bags of cotton, packed by hand, presses not being known, these merchants would buy it and store it in their back yards. There were no ware-houses in those days.

Montgomery was composed of a good class of peo-ple to begin with; they were as a rule moral and sober, notwithstanding they could buy whiskey for twenty-five cents a gallon. There was very little fighting and killing, only two cases of killing at that early period. About the year 1826 a man by the name of Coleman Williams killed a man named Silas Goree. Williams was tried, convicted and hung. The execution took place in an old field back of the Capitol. The next white man hung in Montgomery was James Harkins; he killed a man name Boagly. They were the only two white men ever hung in Montgomery county by sentence of law.

At a still later date the lands surrounding Montgomery and throughout the county began to be taken up very rapidly, both by entry and by purchase, by a very superior class of people, who made money rapidly. They were as a rule wealthy planters, who planted on a large scale. There were in the hands of these planters thousands of dollars,

but it did not go to Montgomery, it went to North
and South Carolina and Virginia to buy negroes,
and to Kentucky and Tennessee to buy mules. The
cotton was shipped to Mobile and New Orleans, and
the merchants in Montgomery did not have a
chance to buy and speculate on the cotton; and
while the city began to build up with larger business
firms and to do a good business, yet it may sound
strange to say that Montgomery was a poor place to
sell goods, as compared to the present time, but such
is the case. No merchant or firm of merchants, before the war, were ever known to become rich. The
law required the merchants to list the amount of
goods sold from January to January, and fifty thous-
and dollars was the largest amount ever returned by
one firm. The planters and farmers made everything at home except flour, sugar and coffee, and
their store accounts were comparatively small.

There are houses on Commerce street at this time, that sell as much in thirty days as the largest houses sold in twelve months in the early days.

Montgomery was more of a place of residence than a place of business. It very soon began to build up with an excellent class of people who had erected fine family residences, and lived with their families in ease and comfort; and no city or town can boast of better society than Montgomery has always had.

Montgomery was noted at an early day for her professional men. The bar was well represented from the earliest day and has had a splended array of legal talent, viz: Moseley Baker, Joseph Hutchison, Thomas Williams, Isaac W. Hayne, John A. Campbell, James E. Belser, John H. and Robert D. Thorington, Nat Harris, Henry Goldthwaite, George

Goldthwaite, W. B. Moss, E. Y. Fair, H. W. Hilliard, W. L. Yancy, M. A. Baldwin, S. F. Rice, T. J. Judge, and others.

The medical profession has been equally as well represented by the following distinguished names, to-wit: Dr. S. D. Holt, Dr. Ames, Dr. J. Marion Sims, Dr. Hinckle, Dr. H. W. Henry, Dr. Brown, Dr. Lucas, Dr. W. O. Baldwin, and others.

At a later day the business houses began to increase, and among the dry goods merchants were the firms of Caffey, Bell & Gilmer, and Pond & Converse, and William Knox, and among the grocery firms were Sayre & Smith and Nicholas & Hutchison, and others.

The first Baptist church that was organized in the city was composed of John Gindrat, Dr. McWhorter, Fred. and William Larkins, and others.   Mr. Gindrat and Dr. .McWhorter were the pillars of the church, and they were superior men in every respect.

The Fork.

Commencing at the confluence or junction of the rivers and going up the Tallapoosa river fifteen or twenty miles, to the Indian line, thence up the Coosa river a few miles, thence a due east line to the Indian line again, thence south along the Indian line to the Tallapoosa river, and you have that portion of Montgomery county known at one time as the Fork. The lands on the Tallapoosa river were of the finest quality; the second bottoms was not so rich, but very level and quite productive; and still higher up from the river is a range of red hills, and at the top of these hills is a beautiful plot of level lands called table lands, very productive and easily cultivated. The wealthier class of farmers owned river plantations, and lived on these beautiful table lands. The Fork seemed to be the favorite portion of the county of the early settlers. These lands were settled by men from Georgia, South and North Carolina and Virginia—principally by Georgians. There were no railroads in those days, and when they left their old homes and came to the new State of Alabama, they moved by land in two, four and six-horse wagons and ox teams; and when they came they brought with them their families, their property, their morals, their religion and politics, and to a great extent they retained their religion and politics to the end.

Among the very earliest settlers of the Fork were the Wilkinsons, Taylors, Simmons, Thompsons, Westmorelands, Adkins, Butlers, Townsends, and others, who had preceded the writer. It is unnecessary to mention these good families in detail.

Suffice it to say that they were a sober, moral, industrious and law-abiding people, that cleared the first lands, belted the first timber, built the first houses and fences, established the first schools and churches and opened the way to a grand future for Montgomery county.

DR. MITCHELL.

Dr. Mitchell, one of these early settlers, was a man in fine circumstances, and was prominent and popular in his vicinity. His plantation was situated on the river, and he lived on one of these tables and was surrounded with every comfort of life. His wife was the daughter of Solomon Wood, sister of Major Green Wood, and grand aunt of Dr. M. L.

Wood, of Montgomery. Mrs. Mitchell was one of the noblest women of her day; she was loved and respected by rich and poor for her great charity and kindness. To show the great love the people had for Mrs. Mitchell, at one time a runner came and reported that the Indians were marching to attack the whites, the whole country was in a state of excitement, and the wife of one poor fellow was hanging on to him and crying, and he said to her, "Be quiet; I know I can't take you to Heaven, but I can take you to Mrs. Dr. Mitchell." That man thought if he could get his wife and children under the protection of Mrs. Mitchell, they would be free from the tommy-hawk and scalping knife.

They had a large family of children: Solomon, John W., Red, Columbus, Thomas and Thwett were the names of their sons. Martha, Mary, Louise and Sarah were the names of their daughters. Solomon never married; John W. married Rebecca Burch, a beautiful girl, daughter of John Burch in the Mt. Meigs neighborhood. Red died quite young. Columbus married a daughter of Phillip Fitzpatrick in the Line Creek neighborhood. Martha, the oldest daughter, married Young Ware, who lived but a little while, and then she married Bennett Griffin. Mary married John Thrasher, a splendid young man. Louise married William Fitzpatrick, and Sarah, the youngest, married a Mr. Cook. Capt. John W. Mitchell, of Mt. Meigs, and Phillip F. Mitchell, of Snowdoun, are grand sons of Dr. and Mrs. Mitchell.

BENJAMAN B. LAMAR.

Benjaman B. Lamar came to the Fork at an early day, and purchased a river plantation, and moved his family and property from Jones county, Georgia, and built a fine residence on one of these tables. He was a man of considerable wealth and influence, and belonged to the distinguished Lamar family of Georgia. He had an interesting young family, but lived only a few years, died very suddenly, respected as a gentleman and christian by every one that knew him. His brother, the Hon. Henry G. Lamar, administered on the estate, sold the plantation and carried the family and negroes back to Georgia.

THOMAS BARTON.

Another grand old man was here in advance named Thomas Barton. He was a man in good circumstances but not rich. He had an interesting family of sons and daughters. His oldest son, Conway, married Martha Cox. John R., familiarly called Jack, married a daughter of Chappel Sledge ; one daughter married a Baptist minister named Daniel; another daughter married Thomas Zimmerman. Mr. Barton was a good man, good neighbor and good citizen, and lived to a ripe old age.

THOMAS HAYNES.

Thomas Haynes, another of the old pioneers, was here in advance. He owned a large plantation on the river, and like the balance of his neighbors, built his residence on the hills above. He had two sons and five daughters. His oldest son, Albert Gallatin, was one of the best young men of his day; he was a useful citizen and member of the Baptist church;

he married a Miss Freeman.   His oldest daughter married a man by the name of Albert Board; the next, Rebecca, married William Maxey, and the next, Harriet, married Abe Autry. Mr. Haynes afterwards sold out, and emigrated to Mississippi, where he died.

———

DR. ROBERT J. WARE

Dr. Robert J. Ware settled in the Fork about the year 1825. He was a rich, talented young bachelor, a practicing physician, a large planter, politician and prominent member of the Baptist church. Dr. Ware was a good citizen and neighbor, and was very charitable with his means; he never hesitated for a moment to extend a helping hand to the needy

or distressed.   He lived a bachelor for several years
and then married a Miss White from Mobile.   He
built a splendid residence on one of these tables
above the river, and was surrounded with every
comfort and convenience for country life.   He had
a park, stocked with deer, the only one ever seen by
the writer.   He belonged to the old Whig party,
and was very popular.   He was the second man
from the Fork that represented Montgomery county
in the Legislature.   Dr. Ware had three children,
two sons and one daughter.   Robert Y., James and
Mary were the names of the children.   Robert married a Miss Molton, James married a Miss Stokes,
the daughter married T. J. Molton, a young lawyer.
The Dr. lived in the Fork a number of years and
then moved to the city and had a fine brick residence there, where he lived the remaining years of
his life.

GREEN WOOD.

Green Wood was a man of wealth, education and influence, and was an early settler. His plantation was on the river, and he lived on the second bottom at a beautiful place between the river and the hills above. After remaining in the Fork for a number of years, he sold his plantation to Dr. Ware and bought a plantation on the Augusta ferry road, seven or eight miles from the city, and there he became noted as the best farmer in the county. He was a great corn planter and raised a variety of corn, known all over the country as the Green Wood corn, and some of that variety of corn is still in existence. Mr. Wood was the father of Maj. Green Wood, of Texas, and grand father of Dr. M. L. Wood, of Montgomery. He sold his beautiful place later on and moved to Texas, and has been dead a number of years.

JOSHUA HAGERTY.

Another of these old pioneers was Joshua Hagerty, a plain, practical, sensible man, in good circumstances. He was a widower, and lived with his children. His residence was situated on the second bottom, and his plantation on the river. Game, his oldest son, married Bettie Zimmerman. Spire married an Indian girl. One of his daughters married Joseph Harwell. Another married a man named Jeter. Mr. Hagerty was a strong Democrat and Dr. Ware was a strong Whig, and while they were neighbors and good personal friends, they did not get along well politically.

BERNARD YOUNG.

Bernard Young was a good pious old methodist preacher; he was a man in easy circumstances, and did the preaching for his neighbors. He commanded the respect of his fellowman for his true worth and merit. He was the father of Bolling Young, who lived and died a bachelor at a good old age, and also of Bernard, better known as Brigham, the late Auctioneer of the city. One of his daughters married Gus Sledge, and another married Hanibal Kavanaugh, and the youngest married a man named Williams.

LARKIN CLEVELAND.

Another early settler was Larkin Cleveland. He was a politician, and a Democrat, and very popular with his party. They had some politics in those early days, as was stated in the outset, and they held to their principles to the end. Mr. Cleveland was the first man from the Fork that represented Montgomery county in the Legislature. He had a nice family of sons and daughters. One daughter married Ebenezer Pond, a man of some note.

CHAPPEL SLEDGE.

Chappel Sledge was a splendid citizen and gentleman. He was a man of fine property. He had a large river plantation and lived with his family out on one of the level tables, and was a very successful planter. He had two sons, Nathaniel and Augustus, and several daughters. One daughter married Isaac Ross. Another married William Ross (two sisters married two brothers). Another daughter married Lucian Pinckston from the other side of the river. William Ross died when comparatively a young man. Isaac Ross lived to a good old age. They were excellent men, and belonged to one of the best families of the county.

AARON LIVINGSTON.

Aaron Livingston, a gentleman from Green county, Georgia, settled with his family in the Fork at an early day. He was a man of wealth, energy and enterprise, and a good farmer. He did not remain long in the Fork, but sold out and moved with his family to Louisiana where he died at a good old age. He was an uncle of Hon. L. F. Livingston, Congressman from Georgia, and grand father of Mrs. W. A. Malloy, of Montgomery county.

MR. BULLARD.

Another of these old settlers was Mr. Bullard.
He lived a few miles above the junction and was a
good farmer, and owned a valuable plantation. He
had a large family of sons and daughters. Henry,
his oldest son, married a daughter of Daniel Moseley,
over the river.   Joseph, his other son, married a
widow, the daughter-in-law of Cotton Seed Moseley,
also on the other side of the river.   Called "Cotton
Seed" because of having at one time sold cotton
seed to a neighbor, a thing never heard of, and ever
after that he was dubbed and called Cotton Seed
Moseley. If a farmer did not have a sufficient
quantity of seed to plant his crop, all he had to do
was to send his wagon to his neighbor's gin-house
and help himself to what he wanted. Mr. Bullard
lived to a ripe old age and died respected by all who
knew him.

PARKER GRAY.

Parker Gray was another good citizen and early settler in the Fork. He owned a plantation above the junction and was a good farmer. He owned a ferry on the Tallapoosa river known as Gray's ferry, and all that portion of citizens, when they wished to cross the river, crossed at Gray's ferry. Mr. Gray has one son still living in this county—Parker Gray, of Pine Level, a good citizen and useful man.

MR. ROSS.

At a very early day in the history of Montgomery county, a gentleman by the name of Ross (his first name is not remembered) settled in the western portion of the Fork. He was from South Carolina and was a man of wealth and of the very highest respectability, and was inferior to no man of his day. He had a splendid family of sons and daughters. His sons, Isaac and William, who married daughters of Chappell Sledge, have been mentioned. His oldest daughter married a man of wealth in South Carolina by the name of Taylor. Mr. Taylor did not live long, and after his death, Mrs. Taylor, with her two children, returned to her father. In due course of time Mrs. Taylor married Henry Lucas, the wealthiest planter in the State at that time. The next daughter married Ben Chappell. The next daughter, Parthinia, married Charles Crommelin, a brilliant young man from the North. He entered in the mercantile business and had a store near where Wetumpka now stands, known then as the falls of the Coosa. He traded with the settlers and the Indians and made money rapidly. After a few years he closed his mercantile business and engaged in planting, and succeeded in that business; and still later on he studied law and was admitted to the bar, and formed a co-partnership with George C. Ball, under the firm name of Ball & Crommelin. Mr. Crommelin still continued to make money. He seemed to have foresight enough to know what the future of Montgomery would be, and he invested his money in Montgomery real estate; and when he died, at not a very advanced age, he left a very handsome fortune to his children. He was the father of the Hon. John G. Crommelin, Mayor of the city, and of Henry Crommelin and Mrs. Dan Robinson. Mr. Ross lived to a good old age.

JOHN ROBERTSON.

And still another of these old pioneers was John Robertson. He emigrated with his family from Putnam county, Georgia, about the year 1822. He was a Baptist minister and a farmer, but did not devote much time to his farm. He was popular with his church and his fellow-citizens, and was elected on two occasions to a lucrative position but afterwards declined official honors. He was a preacher by profession and gave the best and all the years of his life to his Master's cause. After remaining in the Fork a number of years, he sold out and moved and settled in the Line Creek neighborhood, where he remained a number of years; and still later on he moved and settled near Robertson X Roads, where he remained eight or ten years. His church work about this period was very laborious, and he was absent from home four or five days in the week. This hard work caused his health to decline, and he began to age rapidly. On account of his feebleness he moved with his wife (his children all having long since grown up and married) to

2

Macon county, where he could be nearer his church work. He remained there until his wife died and then broke up house-keeping, and lived among his children and friends the remainder of his life— preaching to the end. He was familiarly known as Uncle Jackie, and during an active ministry for over forty years, it is reasonable to conclude that he preached more sermons and funerals, baptized more persons and married more couples, than any other man that ever lived in Montgomery county. He was for a number of years Moderator of the Alabama Baptist Association, the highest official position known to the Baptist church. His wife was Sarah Harris. She was one year older than her husband. She was his constant counselor and adviser, and as her husband was absent from home most of the time the care and responsibility of the family devolved upon the wife and mother, and well did she perform that duty. This old couple reared seven children, five sons and two daughters, and they are all dead except the oldest, (the writer of this little book), still living at the age of 82 years.

———

THE GIN SHOP.

The first Cotton Gin Shop established in Montgomery county, was by a man named James Rogers. His gins were very rudely constructed; everything had to be made by hand. These gins, however, gave very good satisfaction, and James Rogers contributed his share towards building up the new country. The ginning was done altogether by horse power. Small grist mills were established on the streams, and the mills were run by water. There was no steam machinery in those primitive days.

HAROGATE SPRINGS.

There is a mineral spring in the northwest portion of the Fork, called Harogate Springs, and at one time Harrogate Springs was a popular place of resort. Some of the wealthy farmers in the surrounding country built a nice little village of cottages, and spent the summers there with their families; but they soon discovered that the country was sufficiently healthy without the aid of mineral water, and the place has long since been abandoned.

———

These old

SETTLERS AND CITIZENS OF THE FORK

had a little territory of their own. They were, as it seemed, isolated and cut off from the balance of the county; by the Tallapoosa river on the south, the

Coosa on the west, and the Indian territory on the east. They had very little communication with the outside world, but whenever it was necessary to cross the river to Augusta or Montgomery on business, they had ample facilities for crossing. There were Campbell's ferry, Mitchell's ferry, Ware's ferry, Augusta ferry, Judkins' ferry, and Gray's ferry, scattered along up and down the river. There were three things those good people had no need for—a sheriff, a jail, and court-house. If a sheriff crossed the river, it was only to summon some of those good men to serve on the jury. There were no public schools at that time—a free school was not thought of. Each father had to pay for his children's tuition. They kept good schools in their respective neighborhoods and employed good teachers, and gave their children good business educations at home. The boys when not at school were engaged in some useful employment on their father's plantation, and the girls assisted their mothers in the house. There is not an instance on record where a man was killed in the Fork during these early days, or where a son or daughter brought shame or disgrace to themselves or their parents.

These people as a rule were a religious people, and whenever a preacher had an appointment at one of their churches, school-houses or bush-arbors, he did not have to preach to empty benches. He had a congregation every time. There were no carriages, buggies, surreys or dog-carts in those days. People went to church in wagons, on horseback and on foot. Horse blocks were all around the churches for ladies to mount and dismount from their fine horses. If a young man wanted to take a ride with his sweetheart, he had to take it on horseback. The girls were experts in the saddle.

Those early citizens are all dead long since, and if their posterity have not followed in the footsteps of their fathers and mothers, it is their own fault—it was not for the want of proper precept and example. Now let us bid farewell to the Fork and its noble dead and cross the river with our little history.

MT. MEIGS.

Mt. Meigs was first known as Mt. Pleasant. Mc-Dade and Bynum were the first merchants at the place, and afterward a man by the name of Meigs moved there and engaged in merchandizing, and from that time to the present the place has been called Mt. Meigs. At a still later day Frank Wadsworth and others were engaged in business there and it was a business little place. One of its first settlers was Col. Cleman Freeney, a very prominent and popular citizen.

JOHN BURCH.

One of the very earliest settlers in the Mt. Meigs neighborhood was John Burch. He settled a plantation on the Line creek road, between Line creek. and Mt. Meigs. Mr. Burch was a highly respected citizen and gentleman, and had a large family of children. His oldest daughter married Andrew Murdoc, a splendid gentleman and citizen, the father of LaFayette Murdoc, living near Mt. Meigs. The next daughter married John W. Mitchell, previously mentioned. The youngest daughter married a young man named Campbell Williams. One of the sons married a daughter of George Thompson. Mr. Burch lived to a very advanced age.

WALTER B. LUCAS.

One of the earliest settlers was Walter B. Lucas. He had a large ginnery and store on the banks of Line creek. He did an extensive business, trading with the settlers and Indians, and did the ginning for the whole country, and would buy the cotton if the farmers wanted to sell. In a few years he sold out and moved away. Bevery Lucas, brother to Walter B., was killed by the Indians.

———

HENRY LUCAS.

Henry Lucas moved from Georgia and settled a valuable plantation on the Tallapoosa river, not far from Mt. Meigs. When he left Georgia he was badly involved with debt to a bank called Daryan, but he soon settled with the bank and then commenced to make money very rapidly. He added land to land and negroes to negroes, and when he died he was the richest planter in the State. He had five sepa-

rate plantations and probably as many hundred negroes. His plantations were known as the lower
and upper Tallapoosa river plantations, the King
plantation, the Line creek plantation and the Macon
plantation, and a beautiful residence and homestead
at Mt. Meigs. Mr. Lucas married a widow, Mrs.
Taylor, daughter of Mr. Ross, as has been noticed in
a previous chapter. She had two children by her
first marriage. Before Mr. Lucas died he willed each
separate plantation and everything on it, including
negroes, stock, etc., as follows : He willed his lower
river place to his wife's grand children, the Charles.
The upper place, and the homestead at Mt. Meigs,
he gave to James H. Judkins, his nephew. The
King place he gave to Augustus Smith, who married
a relative. The Line creek place he gave to Dr.
Freeny, and his Macon county place to John Judkins.
These parties are all dead except Augustus Smith
and W. T. Charles.

Mr. Lucas was a very eccentric and peculiar man in some respects. His sister had a very valuable plantation on the river, known as the Judkins Ferry place. She had three sons, Tom, John and James Judkins, and when she died the place was valued at sixty thousand dollars. The sons could not agree upon a settlement. Mr. Lucas interfered, and asked Tom what he would take for his interest in the estate and he told his uncle he would take twenty thousand. His uncle gave him a check for the amount. He then asked John what he would take, and John replied that he would take the same, and his uncle gave him a check; and then turning to James, he said: "Now, Jimmy, I give it all to you." James was the favorite nephew of his uncle and transacted all of his uncle's financial affairs. Mr. Lucas died at a good old age. He had no children.

THE McDADE BROTHERS.

There were four brothers from Georgia by the name of McDade who settled in the immediate neighborhood of Mt. Meigs—Charles, Alexander, James and William. They were not wealthy, but were in easy circumstances and were regarded as among the best citizens of the country. Charles has two sons living. Aleck and James have no children living. William McDade owned one of the prettiest places in the Mt. Meigs neighborhood. He was the father of Dr. George W. McDade of the city.

GREEN PINKSTON.

Green Pinkston, one of the first settlers, was a member of the Baptist church and lived in the vicinity of old Antioch church, and had his membership there. He was a strong supporter of his church and was a man that was respected by every one who knew him. Mr. Pinkston had a family of four sons and three daughters. James, one of his sons, married a Miss Mosely. Franklin, a splendid young man, married a Miss Hopper, and John married a Miss Ray. Ann, the oldest daughter, married John Harper. Dolly, the next, married Frank Howard, a good citizen and farmer. Evelin, the youngest, married William McLemore. Mr. Pinkston lived to a ripe old age and gently passed from earth.

JOHN AND ISAAC RAY.

At an early day two brothers, John and Isaac Ray, settled near Mt. Meigs. John Ray was a leading member of the Baptist church and no man commanded more respect in the vicinity where he lived. He was honest and upright in all his dealings with his fellow man, and his word was his bond. His brother, Isaac, was also a good man and citizen. They had each a handsome property.

———

DRS. BROWN, BARTON, LUCAS AND BLAKEY.

Thomas Brown, David Barton, Charles S. Lucas and Bolling Blakey, were the practicing physicians of that time. They were eminent Drs. in their day, and practiced in the whole surrounding country. Dr. Barton and Dr. Lucas never married—lived bachelors all their lives. Dr. Brown had an interesting family and was a man of fine property. Major Thomas W. Oliver married the only daughter of Dr. Brown. Thomas, his oldest son, was killed in battle during the late war. Dr. Blakey married a daughter of David Talliferro. He lived and practiced medicine in the Mt. Meigs neighborhood a number of years and then moved with his family to Macon county and settled on a beautiful plantation near Cross Keys, where he spent the remainder of his life. He was a christian gentleman, highly esteemed by his neighbors. He was the father of Col. David T. Blakey, of Montgomery.

THE McLEMORE BROTHERS.

Three brothers, James, William and Jesse McLemore, at a very early day, settled between Mt. Meigs and Montgomery. James was a Baptist minister of considerable character and influence. He was the second Baptist preacher in the county at that time, Isaac Suttle being the first. William had a beautiful place near old Elam church, with a comfortable property and nice family of children. Jesse also had a plantation and was a man of family. Those McLemore Brothers were good and useful men in that day and generation.

JAMES PINKSTON.

Another gentleman by the name of James Pinkston, an early settler on the Lime creek road, was a man respected as a citizen and neighbor. He was a man in comfortable circumstances, though not rich. One of his sons, Lucian, married a daughter of Chappel

Sledge, over the river. The other son, Sidney, married Margaret Green, daughter of Moses T. Green. One daughter married Jonathan Farley. This daughter died soon after marriage, and then Mr. Farley married a sister of the former wife.

JOHN ASHURST.

A gentleman by the name of John Ashurst, from Putnam county, Georgia, moved to this county at an early day and bought a plantation on the Line creek road. He was a man of considerable wealth. He married a Miss Hill, from Putnam county, before he left Georgia. He had an elegant family of intelligent and moral children. One of his sons, Merrill,

3

was the most accomplished young man of his day. When quite a youth he delivered a fourth of July oration at Mt. Meigs, which gave him considerable notoriety. He afterwards went to California, and there became very popular and was elected or appointed judge of one of their courts. One of Mr. Ashurst's daughters married Hugh Caffey, one of Montgomery's best young men.

———

DAVID TALLIFERRO.

David Talliferro, one among the best men Montgomery ever had, settled at an early day in the prairies, four or five miles from Mt. Meigs. He had a very fine plantation and was quite wealthy, and very popular with his neighbors and friends. One of Mr. Talliferro's daughters married Dr. B. R. Jones and another married Dr. Bolling Blakey. Mr. Talliferro was the grandfather of David Talliferro Blakey, as before mentioned.

JOHN AND JOSEPH GREEN.

Two brothers, John and Joseph Green, settled at an early day in the prairies in the Talliferro neighborhood. They were men in easy circumstances; were members of the Methodist church, and active supporters of church and state. They were prominent men in their day. They were half brothers of James A. Ware.

THOMAS M. COWLES.

Thomas M. Cowles, another old citizen of Montgomery county, was a man of large wealth and influence.   He had a desirable plantation and family residence about five miles from the city, on the Line creek road.   He was one among the most perfect gentlemen in the county, and a man who commanded the respect of all who knew him.   He married a sister of Dr. Robert J. Ware; they had no children. Mr. Cowles died at not an advanced age, honored and esteemed by the whole country.   Mrs. Cowles, some years after the death of her husband, married Col. Edmund Harrison, of the city.

THOMAS VICKERS.

At a very early day a man named Vickers—his first name is not remembered—settled on a fine place about two or three miles from the city, but he did

not live long; and in due course of time Thomas
Vickers married his widow. Thomas Vickers was a
first-class farmer and a good citizen. He lived to a
good old age and died at the old homestead where
he first settled.

GRIFFIN L. HOGAN.

Griffin L. Hogan was another of the early citizens.
He settled on the river flat above the city. He was
a man of moderate circumstances, a good farmer and
citizen in every respect. His wife was a Miss DeBar-
deleben. He had a nice family of children. One
of his daughters married Berry Tatum, of the city.

FELIX ASHLEY.

Felix Ashley, one of Montgomery county's best citizens, had a plantation and beautiful residence below the city. His first wife was a Miss Johnson, daughter of a Protestant Methodist Minister; and after a few years she died. By this marriage he had one son, Augustus, and when about sixteen years of age his father sent him to Tuskegee to school; while there he and a youth by the name of Clay Williams became involved in a boyish fight, when young Williams killed young Ashley; a severe blow to his father. A few years after the death of his first wife he married Miss Ellen Rush, and by this marriage he had several children, who are still at the old homestead. Mr. Ashley died at a good old age.

BEN ASHLEY.

Ben Ashley was a good citizen and a man well to do in the world. He stood high in the estimation of his neighbors and friends. His wife was Mary Nicholson and he had an excellent family. He had a pleasant home and every comfort of life.

WILLIAM FRAZIER.

William Frazier, another early settler, had a fine plantation and residence below the city. He was one of the best farmers in the county and usually sent to market the first bale of cotton of the season. His wife was a Miss Cantelou. They had one son and several pretty daughters who were well educated. Mr. Frazier died at the old homestead.

THE STONE BROTHERS.

Three brothers Barton, Absalom and Warren Stone settled at a very early day west of the city. Barton was the wealthiest of the three. He had a large level plantation, and built the finest brick house in the country and had it handsomely furnished. He sent to New York for his furniture. Fine houses and fine furniture were the exceptions at that day, and Barton Stone's house and furniture attracted a good deal of attention. Mr. Stone was a prominent member of the Methodist church, and his home was the home of all ministers. He built a church upon his own land and kept it up as long as he lived. Mr. Stone was married three times, and raised a splendid family of children. His oldest son, Warren, died in early life. One daughter married John G. Harris, a splendid young man. Dr. Henry L Stone, still living, married a daughter of William Frazier. The other two brothers, Absalom and Warren, were equally as good citizens as their brother, but not so rich. They were also members of the Methodist church, and liberal supporters of the same. They all lived in the same community. As before stated, Barton was married three times, and Absalom married three times and Warren married four times. The three brothers between them had ten wives. Those brothers are all dead, and the old homesteads are still in the hands of their descendants.

CHARLES G. GUNTER.

Charles G. Gunter, a gentleman with his young family and property, moved from North Carolina at an early day and settled a plantation ten miles west of the city, on the east side of Pintlala creek. His wife was Eliza Adams, daughter of Shockley Adams of South Carolina. He was a man of intelligence, energy and enterprise, and was a very prominent and popular man with his people. He was a planter, lawyer and politician, and belonged to the old Whig party, but was liberal in his views. He did not hate his political opponents because they differed with him in politics. He was very popular with his party and a leader in the same. He was elected to the Legislature on several occasions and acquitted himself well. Mr. Gunter accumulated propérty rapidly, and was among the wealthiest men in this county. Mr. Gunter was a strong supporter of the Confederacy, and when the South surrendered and all was lost he determined to leave the United States forever, and as soon as he could make necessary arrangements he bid farewell to his host of friends and his native South and left for Brazil, where he spent the remaining years of his life. Mr. Gunter was the father of Col. W. A. Gunter, Harris Gunter, and Mrs. Frank Elmore of the city. Another one of his sons now lives in Brazil.

KIN MOONY.

About the year 1836 political excitement was at fever heat in this county between the old Whig and Democratic parties. A man would not vote for a personal friend or brother of different political opinions. The militia of the county was well organized. The Generals, Colonels and Captains were elected by direct vote of the people, and during that summer there was a regimental muster held about nine miles south of the city, on the road leading to

Troy.   Col. Thomas Mastin was the commanding officer.   He was a very prominent and popular man; he belonged to the Democratic party and was a leader of the same.   A gentleman by the name of Bush W. Bell and his two nephews, with a party of friends, went out from Montgomery to that muster and carried a tent with them.   They were Whigs and very popular with their party.   When the muster was over Col. Mastin went to the tent of the Bells by invitation, and soon afterwards he and Edward Bell got into a political dispute and fight, in which Bell stabbed and killed Mastin before their friends could separate them.   Mastin was cut down in the full strength of manhood, surrounded by a host of friends and leaving a wife and two children.   This killing was not premeditated; there was no malice or unkind feeling existing between them before the difficulty; it was done in the heat of passion and

without time for reflection. Bell went back to town
and surrendered to Temp Reid, then sheriff of the
county. He gave bond for his appearance at the
next term of the Circuit Court to answer the charge
of murder, and before the trial he and his friends
employed the best legal talent to be found. Col.
Thomas Williams of Mobile, who had the reputation
of being the best criminal lawyer in the state, was
employed as leading counsel, and at the trial Bell
was acquitted. The family and immediate friends
of Mastin did all they could, legally, to secure Bell's
conviction; but failing, and being good and law
abiding men, they let the matter drop. But unfor-
tunately the matter did not stop here. William
Moony, with his family, resided about twenty miles
southeast of the city. He was not in any manner
related to the Mastins. He was a democrat and a
man of high prejudice; he loved his friends and
hated his enemies, and was a man of some prominence in his vicinity. His son Kinion, who was
about the average young man of his day, rather

popular with his associates, accused of no wrong doing, and of good moral character, took an active part in politics, and followed the fortunes of his father. As their political friend had been killed in a political fight, they determined to avenge his death. It is not known whether the Bells had been informed of the intention of the Moonys or not, but when they met, near the old Montgomery Hall, a desperate and deadly fight took place, in which young Bush Bell killed William Moony and Kin Mooney killed Edward Bell (Mastin's slayer). Bell had no family. His body was taken in charge by his friends, there being no undertakers in those days. Moony's body was carried home to his family. Bush Bell left the country and Kin Moony was sent to jail. In a few days Moony's friends made his bond and he was discharged and returned home to his family. In a short time after that a company muster was held at a place called Scoggins Hill, about one mile east of Robertson's X Roads. About noon Mooney rode up and hitched his horse. He walked

quietly up to the crowd armed to the teeth. There
was an old lady on the ground with a cake cart, and
Moony took a position near that cart without speaking to anyone. After the muster was over, a man
by the name of Allister Owens went up to the cart
to buy some cakes. Moony, without any cause or
provocation, walked up to that man and stabbed him
to death. When Owens was seen to fall some one
cried out to go for a doctor. Moony remarked that
if they brought a doctor there he would kill him.
In a few minutes he mounted his horse and rode
deliberately away, as if nothing had happened. No
one tried to arrest or stop him; it would have been
death to attempt it. Owens was a quiet and inoffensive man, and no one knew any reason why
Moony should want to kill him. Every one expected
that Moony would leave the country, but he did no
such thing. He went back home, and when it was
learned that he had not left, a bench warrant was
issued for his arrest, charging him with murder in
the first degree. The warrant was placed in the

hands of the sheriff who placed it in the hands of his most trusted deputy, and a large posse of the best citizens of Montgomery, instructing them to arrest Moony and bring him in dead or or alive.

Some of Moony's friends learned that the sheriff and posse were getting ready to make the arrest, and they informed him immediately. Moony was at his mother's house. He barricaded the doors and windows and prepared for a seige. When the sheriff and posse arrived they demanded of him to come out and surrender, but he sent them word he would do no such thing, and the first man that put his foot inside that yard would be killed on the spot, and they knew he meant what he said. They were at their wit's end. To attempt to force an entrance would be death to some of them, and to go back to town and report to the sheriff that he was in his mother's house and that they could not arrest him, would not do; so they held a council, and decided to send back to town for a cannon and ammunition to blow the house down, and give the inmates the choice of coming out or remaining in as they saw proper. They selected Phillip Raiford and Theodrick Ruddle to go back for the cannon. They procured the cannon and ammunition, and mounted it on a wagon and started for the seat of war. Some of Moony's friends learned that the cannon was coming, and they waylaid the road and when near the house they fired into the wagon and badly wounded Raiford, made the horses run away, and scared Ruddle nearly to death; and in the confusion and excitement that followed Moony escaped and made for the swamp. Those men were not to blame. They were not expecting anything of the kind, and there was nothing left to do but to take their wounded and the cannon back to town and report to the sheriff.

The next news of Moony, he was in the southwestern portion of the county. There was a volunteer military company in the county with about sixty members called the Prairie Invincibles. The warrant was placed in the hands of the Captain of that com-

4

pany, and he was ordered to arrest Moony or run
him out of the country. The Captain detailed sixteen of his best men, and they assembled at the appointed place of meeting, armed and mounted.
About sundown they started in pursuit of Moony.
There never was a brighter moonlight night or a
more serious looking set of fellows. They first
searched in the neighborhood of what is now known
as Ramer, making inquiries; afterwards they went
in the direction of Tucker's precinct, and there
they learned that in all probability he could be
found at the house of Dick Colbert, who was living
about four miles from Tucker's, in the direction of
Pintlala creek. Colbert was a bachelor living by
himself, and a man of some property. On their route
to Colbert's house two or three of the men straggled
or got behind. In all armies there are more or less
stragglers, and so it was in this case. In approach-
ing Colbert's house there was a lane, and on the side
of the lane there was a gin-house and old-fashioned
wood screw, and about one hundred and fifty yards

below the gin was the dwelling. When they rode
up to the screw there were two negro fellows sitting
under it, and when asked if there was any body at
the house they said, Yes, Mr. Kin Moony and Mr.
Charley Spratt were at the house, and they hurriedly
turned the screw. The Captain ordered his men to
dismount quickly and surround the house on foot,
but the turning of the screw was the signal of dan-
ger, and before the men could get in position Moony
and Spratt ran out of the house and mounted their
horses which were standing hitched, bridled and
saddled, in the yard. They passed through the gate
and out of the lane at full speed and made good their
escape. The Captain ordered his men to fire; eight
or ten shots were fired at them, but without effect—
neither of them were hurt. Moony lost his hat which
was kept as a trophy.

He realized then and there that he was an outlaw,
and that he would have to surrender or leave the
country, and that night was the last ever heard of
Kin Moony. His family and friends never heard of

him again—where he went has never been known.
He had some good traits of character; he loved his
family, he loved his friends, and if his hands had
not been stained with human blood, he might have
made a good and useful citizen.

GEORGE THOMAS.

Another of the old citizens was George Thomas.
He moved with his family and property from North
Carolina, and bought a plantation from James Blair
Gilmer, below the city.   His wife was Mary Adams,
sister of Mr. Charles G. Gunter.   Mr. Thomas was
strictly a planter, and very successful as such; he
made money very rapidly.   He lived a few years on
his plantation, then bought a lot in the village of
Lowndsboro and built a fine family residence where
he moved with his family and lived the remainder
of his life.   His wife survived her husband a number

of years and died at a ripe old age, loved and respected for her pure life and christian character. They had a number of children, but they are all dead except one daughter, Mrs. Moore, who lives with her husband in one of the Western States.

ABNER McGEHEE.

Abner McGehee, at a very early day, settled in Montgomery county at a place now known as McGehee's Switch. He owned a large plantation and was a man of wealth, energy and enterprise. He was looked upon by all who knew him as one among the very best men in the county. He was a good citizen and neighbor, a kind husband and father, and a humane master to his slaves. He was a member of the Protestant Methodist Church and was an active church supporter. His christian character was early formed; it was a character of strength and

earnestness. One of the most distinctive qualities
of Mr. McGehee's christian character was his modesty.
He went about doing good, but was never heard to
boast of any good thing he ever did; his text was,
'let not thy left hand know what thy right hand
doeth.' His resignation was a beautiful trait; he
was never heard to murmer or complain, but on the
contrary was always pleasant, affable and agreeable
in manner. He donated to the American Bible Society the house known as the Bible House, in order
that the society might have a branch of its business
in Montgomery. Mr. McGehee had a splendid family
of sons and daughters. Abner, his oldest son, married a daughter of James Smith. James, another
son, married Rachael Daily, daughter of Dr. Daily.
The youngest son was killed by a stroke of lightning
while riding through his father's plantation. One
of his daughters was the wife of (Brickhouse) William
Taylor. Another daughter married Dr. Sam C.
Oliver; another was the wife of Mr. Jarrett. The

next married Dr. Briggs; he did not live long, and then she became the wife of the genial and intelligent James G. Gilchrist; and another married Mr. Graves. A daughter of this last marriage is the wife of the progressive farmer and planter, A. H. Clark, living now at the old homestead.

DAVID CALLOWAY.

David Calloway, another of these old settlers, moved from Georgia and settled on the Mobile road, twelve miles south of Montgomery. Mr. Calloway was a successful farmer, and was a man that was highly respected for his many good qualities. He reared a large family, three sons and six daughters. John B. Calloway, of Snowdoun, is his oldest son. The other two sons died in early manhood. One of Mr. Calloway's daughters is the wife of William C. Mason; another married Thomas Davis; another married Mr. Hays; another married Clark Taylor; another married James Taylor (brothers); and another married Scovil Battle. Mr. Calloway lived to a good old age and died at the old homestead about the year 1851.

———

COLONY FROM GEORGIA.

At an early day a small colony emigrated from Oglethorpe county, Georgia, and settled in the eastern portion of Montgomery county. Their names were William Barnett, Thomas Barnett, two Nat Barnetts, Frank Barnett and Charles Barnett, Francis M. and David Gilmer, little George and big George Mathews, Dr. Mathews, Graves Howard, Thomas DeYampert, Nicholas Marks and Dr. Nicholas Meriweather. All these families were more or less related and they entered in a body a very large amount of that rich praire land. The land office at that time was in Cahaba, and they paid the Government one dollar and a quarter per acre. Land could be entered in quantities not less than eighty acres up to thousands of acres, and these settlers embraced the opportunity that made their own and their children's fortune. After those lands had been once put in a state of cultivation they were very easy to cultivate. A very large per cent was what is called "bald praire," and the timbered portion was comparatively easy to clear; there was no under growth—nothing but large trees; a deer could be seen a quarter of a mile through the woods. The average crop of these lands was about a bale of cotton per acre, corn about forty bushels, and these planters grew rich rapidly. These citizens will be mentioned one at a time:

THOMAS M. BARNETT.

Thomas M. Barnett was the richest man among them. He owned a large body of land and slaves and other property in proportion. He was a man

of extraordinary energy and business qualities.   As
an instance of his energy :   On one occasion, in the
month of January, his overseer, Ross Harris, called
at the big house (as it was called in those days)
after supper and told Mr. Barnett that in order to
prepare the land properly he would need about
twelve more mules.   Mr. Barnett got up about 2
o'clock next morning, took a couple of negro boys
with him, and went to town, a distance of fifteen or
sixteen miles, bought the mules, brought them home
and had them hitched to the plow before dinner.
(This incident was told the writer by Harris himself.)
That was Mr. Barnett's way of doing business.   His
wife was a Miss Micou.   He was a kind husband
and father and a good citizen.   Mr. Barnett at a
later day purchased the water power at what was
known as the Falls of the Tallapoosa, and built a
large cotton factory and named it Tallassee.   That
factory is still in operation.   Mr. Barnett only had
three children, two sons, Thomas and Nicholas, and
one daughter, Lucy.   Lucy married Ben Micou, a

cousin. Thomas married a Miss Micou, a cousin.
Nick went out of the family for a wife and married
Sallie Powell, a daughter of George Powell. Mr.
Barnett lived to a good old age and died, leaving his
property to his children.

FRANK BARNETT.

Frank Barnett was a valuable and useful citizen
and stood high in the estimation of his friends and
neighbors. He was very correct in all his dealing
with his fellow man. He was strictly a farmer with
all that the name implies. He made an abundance
of home supplies and was surrounded with every
home comfort. He was fond of hunting and kept a
pack of hounds. Deer were very plentiful in those
days and Mr. Barnett was very fond of the sport and
was always ready to [go driving, as it was called,
which was done in the following manner: Deer

were accustomed to have certain runs or routes, which they never failed to follow when pursued by dogs, and a day would be appointed to have a drive and the hunters would meet at some specified place. A part of the company would station themselves at places along these runs, called stands, while others would take the dogs and go driving. When the deer were jumped or started, they would invariably follow one of these runs at full speed, the dogs and huntsmen after them, and as they passed the stands the report of the guns would be heard, and usually a fine buck and sometimes two or three would be killed. Mr. Barnett, when in pursuit of deer, would never stop for a broken stirrup or girth.

Mr. Barnett's wife was Sarah Ponder. He had several children. He was the father of the Hon. Joel Barnett and grand father of Dr. B. J. Baldwin, of the city.

CHARLES BARNETT.

Charles Barnett, another good citizen, was a brother of Frank Barnett. He had a nice property and family. His wife was a Miss Gresham. He was regarded as one of the most religious men in all the county. The boys used to tell that Charles had a place near his house that he would go to have secret prayer, and that he made a visible path in going to and from that place. A man with that zeal for religion could not help being a good husband and father and useful citizen.

COL. GEORGE MATHEWS,

Better known as little George Mathews, was very wealthy; he was the largest land owner in Montgomery county, except Henry Lucas. He owned about eight thousand acres of land in a body, and a large amount of other property. His first wife was

Rebecca Marks, daughter of Nicholas Marks; she was a general favorite with her family. Mr. Mathews was heard to say on one occasion that whenever one of the family was taken sick, they would always send for "Beck." as he called her. They had no children. Mrs. Mathews died at not an advanced age. After a few years Mr. Mathews married a young lady, Miss Mayhue. There were no children by this marriage. Mr. Mathews lived to a good old age; and before his death he willed all his property to his last wife, who survived her husband a few years, and at her death she willed it to Mrs. Mathews, afterwards Mrs. Forniss, a niece of his first wife and daughter of Gen. James F. Watkins.

BIG GEORGE MATHEWS.

Big George Matthews was also a man of large property in land, negroes and money. He was called big George, as the name implies, to distinguish him from little George. He was universally admired and respected for his many noble qualities, and no man stood higher in the estimation of his fellow men than did Mr. Mathews. He left two sons and one daughter, William B., Miss Fannie and Charles H. William B. married a daughter of William M. Marks. Miss Fannie never married. Charles H. married a daughter of the noble Lorenzo James.

NICHOLAS MARKS.

Nicholas Marks was immensely rich; his property, like most planters, consisted of land, negroes and money. The enhanced value of lands, the natural increase of negroes and stock, the large crops made and the general prosperity of the country in those days, all naturally contributed towards making men rich. Mr. Marks was a very plain and unassuming man, very kind to his neighbors and friends, and was among the very best citizens of his day. He had an excellent and intelligent family of sons and daughters. William, his oldest son, first married a Miss Olive. His second wife was a daughter of the grand old gentleman Spencer Crane, of Georgia. One of Mr. Marks daughters married William B. S. Gilmer, a wealthy and popular gentleman who represented Montgomery county in the Legislature on one or two occasions. Another was the wife of James F. Watkins; another the wife of Gen. Tom Scott, and another the wife of little George Mathews, as before mentioned. Mr. Marks lived to a ripe old age.

JEFF DeYAMPERT.

Jeff DeYampert, in a few years after settling in this county, sold out and moved with his family to Dallas or Marengo county. He was quite a gentleman in every respect. His wife was a northern lady and very intelligent.

DR. NICHOLAS MERIWEATHER.

The writer is not gifted with power of speech to do justice to the character and worth of this good man. He was one of the greatest and grandest men living in Montgomery county in his day. He was wealthy and surrounded by every comfort of life. There was no necessity for performing physical or mental labor, yet this man did what no man ever did before or since. He practiced medicine for the whole surrounding country year after year, without money and without price. He did not do this for popularity or fame; he did not seek notoriety; he had no political or other aspirations to gratify; but he did it through motives of love and sympathy for his people in their season of sickness and suffering. Day after day he went on his round of visiting the sick, and night after night he would sit by the bed-side. The rich and the poor were the recipients of his services alike.

5

Dr. Meriweather was what might be called a self-made man. His education was limited; but by study, practice and experience, he became one of the most successful physicians ot his day, and was honored with diplomas from several of the best medical colleges of the country, although he had never entered a college or attended a lecture. After spending his life in doing good, at a ripe old age he passed from earth, to receive the well merited reward, "well done good and faithful servant." His wife was a Miss DeYampart, and she was a strong supporter of her husband in his good work, and was never heard to murmur or complain on account of the Doctor's absence from home, but gave him her sympathy and encouragement to the end.

They had a family of five sons—no daughters. James, Thomas, George, Nick and William were the names of the sons, and they were the perfection of morality, sobriety and industry. As they grew up to manhood and married, their father would settle them on a plantation and give them a start in life. These sons were all useful citizens in their day, and are now all dead.

DR. SAMUEL C. OLIVER.

Dr. Samuel C. Oliver, an early citizen of Montgomery county, was a man of wealth and influence. He represented his county in the Legislature almost continuously for fifteen or eighteen years, and no man stood higher in the esteem of his fellow citizens than did Dr. Oliver. In politics he was a Whig, in religion he was a Methodist, but conservative and liberal in his views. He was never abusive to his political opponents, but on the stump and in the hustings met their argument with argument. He was educated and a fluent debater. He was popular with his people, and was never defeated. He always signed his name "Sam C. Oliver." His wife was Mildred Mc-

Gehee. They had a splendid family of children, three sons and two daughters. The oldest daughter was born the night the stars fell, as it was commonly called, and she was named Mary Meteora. Major Thomas W. Olver is the only son living. Dr. Oliver was an elder brother of the Rev. Christopher D. Oliver of the Alabama Conference; and still another younger brother was Dr. John A. Oliver, who died in early manhood.

FRANCIS M. GILMER.

Francis M. Gilmer was a model man. He had all the qualities that it takes to constitute the perfect gentleman. He was a good citizen, good neighbor, and good friend. He was a kind husband and father, and an indulgent master to his slaves. The good book says, train up a child in the way he should go and when he is old he will not depart from it, and

Mr. Gilmer came as near complying with that injunction as a man could do, as was demonstrated by his children. They were moral, sober and religious. He had four sons—if any daughters, they are not remembered. W. B. his oldest son married a Miss McGehee. She lived only a few days after marriage; he then married Lncy Early, a daughter of John Gilmer, a relative. Another son, Dr. Frank, married a Miss Green, and George N. married the daughter of Morgan Smith of Lowndes county.

Groves Howard and family, David Gilmer and family, and Nat. Barnett and family, about the year 1834 emigrated from Montgomery county to Noxubee county, Miss., and by that move Montgomery county lost a very superior class of citizens.

PEACHY, W. B. S. AND JAMES J. GILMER.

Three brothers, Peachy, W. B. S. and J. J. Gilmer, moved from Georgia at an early day and settled in a body on the west side of Catoma creek. They were brothers of George R. Gilmer, former Governor of Georgia, and also brothers of Mrs. Judge B. S. Bibb, one of Montgomery's noblest women. They, like others of those early settlers, soon became very rich. Peachy Gilmer was different from all the rest of the Gilmer family; he was impetuous and impulsive, and did not seem to have that confidence in his fellow man that was characteristic of the Gilmer family. In politics he was a Democrat, and he had very little patience with a political opponent. He went to town on one occasion, when politics were running high, and was informed that there was a case of small pox in town. He said it was a lie, a regular Whig lie, and he would not believe it until he saw it for himself. The case was in a room up-stairs, and Mr. Gilmer went deliberately up the steps, opened the door and looked in. In about ten days he had a fully developed, though not serious, case of small pox. Mr. Gilmer's second wife was the widow of Col. Jet Thomas, of military fame. He was the Colonel of a Regiment stationed at Savannah, and was very popular with his Regiment. Mrs. Gilmer was a very superior woman. Notwithstanding Mr. Gilmer's peculiarities, he had a splendid family of children, made so by the influence of a good cristian mother. Thomas, his oldest son, never married. Robert married Mary Murray. Sallie, the oldest daughter, married a Dr. James, a very devout christian. Eliza married James Blair Gilmer, a relative; and Martha, the youngest, married Dr. Gratton, and after his death she married Francis M. Gilmer, Jr.

William B. S. Gilmer was a very popular and prominent man, and was an influential man in his county and a representative in the Legislature, as has been mentioned in a former chapter. He married a daughter of Nicholas Marks; they had no children. After remaining on his plantation a few years, he left it in charge of a superintendent, and moved to LaFayette, Chambers county; there he adopted a boy by the name of Frank Perry. He spent the remaining years of his life there, and at his death willed his property to his wife. She survived her husband only a few years, and at her death willed all her property to the boy Frank, and at his death he willed it back to Mrs. Gilmer's family.

James J. Gilmer had the qualities of his brother William; he was a man that was respected and admired for his many good qualities; he was a kind and indulgent husband and father; he loved his family, loved his neighbors, loved his people, and was himself a lovable man. His wife was Elizabeth Jordan, daughter of Reuben Jordan. They were married fifteen years before they had any children; after which time they had four daughters. His oldest daughter married Dr. Clanton, brother of the lamented Gen. J. H. Clanton. The next married

Dr. Thad Weatherly; the next married a young man named Mills. The youngest died when about fourteen years of age. Mr. and Mrs. Gilmer died at a ripe old age.

MICHAEL ELSBERRY.

Michael Elsberry, another of these old pioneers, moved with his young family from Georgia about the year 1830 and settled on Line creek. After remaining there a few years, he again moved to the Robertson's X Roads neighborhood. As citizen, husband, father, friend and neighbor Mr. Elsberry had few equals and no superiors. He was a devout christian; a member of the Methodist church and a strong supporter of the same. He was liberal and charitable with his means, and ever ready to extend the helping hand to the poor and needy. His wife was Eliza Ponder, and like her husband, was a good christian and member of the Methodist church. She died about the year 1836. They had four children, Benjamin, Foster, Sallie and Lorena. Benjamin married a Miss Boykin; Foster married a daughter of Col, Sam'l L. Arrington; the daughters never married. A number of years after the death of his wife, Mr. Elsberry married Judeth Payne, a beautiful young lady, and by this marriage had three children. Dr. Jno. P. married a daughter of Col. J. R. Dillard; Callie, a daughter, married Julius C. Alford, son of the old war horse of political fame; and Emma, a daughter, married Col. Bradford Dunham.

WILLIAM FALCONER.

William Falconer, at a very early day in the history of Montgomery county, settled on the Mount Meigs road near the city, and afterwards moved to the head waters of Ramer creek. He had a splendid plantation and a very pretty property, and succeeded well as a planter. He was a member of the Presbyterian church and a prominent man in the community. Mr. Falconer had a large family of children. Martha, the oldest daughter, was the wife of Dr. Hugh W. Henry. Nancy, another daughter, was the wife of Benjamin Hart. Sarah, the next, was the wife of Col. J. R. Dillard. Jane, the next, was the wife of Dr. Charles McEachin; and Henrietta, the youngest, was the wife of Peter G. Powell. Mr. Falconer was the grand father of Dr. J. H. Henry, of Montgomery.

WILLIS CALLOWAY.

Willis Calloway, a gentleman from Georgia, settled at first on the river above the city, and for a number of years remained on his plantation at that place. He was a planter and very successful. After the death of his wife, in due time he married the widow of Robert Gilmer and daughter of H. M·

Murray.   Mr. Calloway was a good man and citizen and stood well in the opinion of his friends and neighbors.   After the death of his second wife he discontinued housekeeping and lived among his children, in ease and comfort, the remaining days of his life.   He was the father of Joseph A. Calloway, of Snowdoun.

REUBEN EMERSON.

Reuben Emerson was among the very earliest of these old settlers.   He entered one hundred and twenty acres of land on the Carter's Hill road about two miles east of Robertson X Roads.   Mr. Emerson was county surveyer for a number of years, and stood high in the esteem of all who knew him.   He was a devout member of the Methodist church and was noted for his good christian character.   He was from North Carolina.   His wife was Margarette Karr. They raised a large family of children, five sons and four daughters.   One daughter married Job Thompson, of Macon county. Another married Leander McKenzie. Another married Col Shuford, of Lowndes county. This entire family are all dead, except the oldest son, John Emerson, now a very old man. Mr. and Mrs. Emerson lived to extreme old age and died at the old homestead.

COL. DANIEL MALLOY.

Col. Daniel Malloy moved from North Carolina and settled on the Norman Bridge road, about one mile east of Ramer creek. He was a bachelor in very comfortable circumstances. He was a member of the Presbyterian church, and a kind-hearted and liberal man with his means. He raised and educated two nephews that were prominent men. He lived to a ripe old age and died while on a visit to his old home in North Carolina.

MRS. DELILAH DABNEY.

Aunt Dabney, as she was familiarly known, was born and raised in Oglethorpe county, Georgia. In early womanhood she married Reuben Dillard and they took a bridal tour from Georgia to Virginia on horseback. Mr. Dillard lived only a few years and died, leaving two children, a son and a daughter. Mrs. Dillard afterwards married Capt. William O. Dabney, and about the year 1833 they moved to Montgomery county, and settled in the vicinity of Robertson X Roads. Capt. Dabney only lived a few years and died, loved and respected by his friends and neighbors. After the death of her husband, Mrs. Dabney remained on her plantation and attended to every detail of her business for a period of about forty years. She was a very remarkable woman, and was noted for sound, practical sense and judgment, and was known far and wide for her many excellent traits of character. She went about doing good, visiting the sick, offering words of comfort to the bereaved and distressed, and helping the poor and needy. She was a member of the Presbyterian church and a strong believer in the doctrine of the same. She submitted to the decrees of God with christian resignation, and was never heard to murmer or complain Late in life she removed with her son, Col. James R. Dillard, to the city, where she lived the remaining days of her life. At the age of ninety years she gently passed away, and her remains were laid by the side of her husband in the family burial ground at the old homestead.

A. F. PONDER.

A. F. Ponder, emigrated from Georgia with his young family to Montgomery county, and finally settled on the Norman Bridge road, east of Ramer creek. Mr. Ponder was a planter by occupation, and was considered one of the best in the county. He was a great cotton raiser and made money rapidly. He was a very quiet and unassuming man, attended strictly to his own business, and did not meddle in the affairs of other men. He was very accommodating and obliging to his neighbors, and to a great degree was their banker. He would loan them money at the legal rate of interest, and was never known to press a man for the payment of a debt. After remaing on his plantation a number of years, he moved with his family to the city on account of failing health. His health continued to fail, and he died at not an advanced age. His wife Eliza Borders. They reared a large family of children.

BENAJAH S. BIBB.

Judge B. S. Bibb was among the earliest settlers of Montgomery county. He bought a valuable plantation a few miles south of the city. After a few years he moved with his family to the city. Judge Bibb was a very popular and prominent man with his people. About the year 1834 he was elected State Senator, and subsequently to that time represented his county in the lower house of the Legislature. At a still later period he was elected by the Legisla-ture Judge of the County Court, which position he held for twelve years. In religion Judge Bibb was a Methodist. In politics he was an old line Whig, and a leader in his party. About the year 1854 Pres-ident Fillmore visited Montgomery and was enter-tained at the hospitable home of Judge Bibb, and, in company with Mr. John P. Kennedy, went with the Judge in his carriage to his plantation, where the comfort and the cheerfulness of the slaves, and their attachment to their owner and his family, was a striking contrast with the northern idea of slave life in the south. That visit was a revelation to the President and made a deep impression on him.

His wife was Sophia Gilmer, sister of Gov. George R. Gilmer of Georgia. She was one of the noblest women of her day, and was loved and respected for

6

her excellent christian character and influence. She was a member of the Protestant church and a liberal supporter of the same. The Protestant church in the city stands to-day as a memorial to the christian character of Aunt Sophia Bibb. They lived to celebrate their Golden Wedding and a few years after, and at a ripe old age died. Mrs. Bibb survived the death of her husband only a short time, and she too gently passed away. They both died as they had lived—loved, honored and respected by all who knew them.

RICHARD C. BUNTING.

Richard C. Bunting moved from North Carolina at an early day, and settled in Montgomery county. He was a highly educated man and was very popular in his adopted home. He was a man who would attract attention anywhere, and soon became one of the most prominent men in the county. He engaged in farming when he first settled and was very successful. His first wife was a sister of Gen. McQueen, a distinguished North Carolinian who represented his district in Congress a number of years. By this marriage he had five children, four sons and one daughter. His wife died in early life. He afterwards married the widow of Hector McEachin, and by this marriage he had two children. In a few years he was elected member of the Legislature, and died at his hotel in Tuscaloosa. David J., the oldest son, married Susan Westcott. Thomas, another son, married a daughter of Henry Holmes. McQueen, another son, was killed in Lowndes county by Sam Ivey.

THOMAS CAFFEY.

Thomas Caffey was one of the old pioneers and land marks. He came to the county at an early day, and for fifty years was among the best citizens of his county. No man stood higher in the esteem of his people than did Mr. Caffey. He was a farmer by occupation and lived in the country and among country people all his life. He represented his county in the Legislature on one or two occasions and acquitted himself to the satisfaction of his people. Mrs. Steele, of Ramer, and Mrs. C. R Waller, of Montgomery, are daughters, and Mrs. William C. Ray, of Montgomery, is a grand daughter of Mr. Caffey. He lived to an extreme old age and died at his home near Ramer.

BRYANT WALTERS.

Bryant Walters was another of those old settlers. He entered a home on the west side of Ramer creek, built his house, cleared his field, married his wife and raised his children on that farm, and never moved until his friends carried him to his final resting place. He was a member of the Primitive Baptist church, and was an honest man and good citizen.

DR. P. W. SPEAR.

Dr. P. W. Spear was another of those early settlers. He first lived in the vicinity of Robertson's X Roads. He was a remarkably fine looking young man, and was very popular among his associates. He first married a Miss Gregory, sister of Buck Gregory, who was sheriff of Montgomery county at a very early day. His wife lived only a few years. After a number of years he married a daughter of Hooper Caffey, and by this marriage he had several children. He was at one time in possession of a pretty property, but was unfortunate and lost the greater part of it. He then commenced to study medicine and soon became a very popular and successful practicing physician, and by that means made a very comfortable support for his family. Dr. Spear was a man who commanded the respect of his fellow men all the days of his life. He lived to an extreme old age and gently passed away.

HARDY ROBINS.

Hardy Robins was the first man who settled along the Rocky Mount Road south of the city. It is not remembered what state he emigrated from. He entered from the Government eighty acres of land

and built his house near what is now the Station of
Tharin on the Ala. Midland R. R.   He built the first
house, cleared the first acre of land, belted the first
timber and planted the first apple tree south of
Montgomery.   It could be truthfully said of Mr.
Robins that he never paid a debt, for the reason that
he never made a debt.   His doctrine was pay as you
go, and if you can't pay don't go.   He was a member
of the Hard Shell Baptist church, and his religion
was the "Bible and the Hard Shell Baptist."   He
would occasionally take a little whiskey for his
stomach's sake, but never got drunk.   He was an
inoffensive, good old man, who provided well for his
family and was liked by his neighbors.   A few years
before his death he had his coffin made and "paid
for it."   He kept it under his bed, and when the
final summons came he was ready ; there was nothing
to do but lay him to rest.   After his death the original old sheep-skin title to his land, with the signa-
ture of the Government, was found in his trunk.

JOHN BONHAM.

John Bonham, another of these old citizens, settled at what was known as Bonham's X Roads. He was a first-class citizen in every respect. He raised a large family of children. Two of his daughters married two brothers by the name of Killough. (Beat 10 is known by that name.) Capt. B. J. Bonham, a former citizen, now dead, was a son of John Bonham. Capt. Bonham was a bold Confederate soldier, and he was at home on a furlough just at the close of the war. The Federal raid was passing through the country and Capt. Bonham got together a little squad of men and gave them considerable annoyance. On one occasion a Federal officer with a squad of men got separated from the main army and were scouting around, taking stock, cattle, etc. Capt. Bonham learned of his whereabouts and sent him word by a negro to give him battle. The Yankee captain sent him word to meet him in the road at a certain place. They met in a lane and each squad charged the other, shooting and slashing with their sabers. Nobody was hurt, but the Yankees left the neighborhood. Mr. Bonham lived to a good old age, and died at the old homestead.

GEORGE SHACKELFORD.

George Shackelford, another of these early settlers, was among the best and most useful men of his day. He settled on the west side of Pintlala creek. He had a very comfortable property, though not rich. He was a very enterprising man, a good farmer and citizen. He was a strong believer in the Baptist church and a liberal supporter of the same. By his energy and influence he had built on his own land one of the first Baptist churches in the county, and old Bethel stands to-day as a memorial to the character and enterprise of George Shackelford. Mr. Shackelford lived to a good old age, and when he died he left a legacy besides his property. He left a splendid family of sons and daughters to perpetuate his name and memory. His oldest son, Wash, married a Miss Delbredge. Frank married a Miss Watts. Matt married a Miss Ledbetter. One daughter was the wife of Nathaniel Williams. Another was the wife of William L. Allen. Another is the wife of W. W. Walker, and the youngest is the wife of W. S. Stokes.

HENRY HOLMES.

Henry Holmes was an early inhabitant. He was a good citizen in every respect and a member of the Baptist church. He was very rich and was a large money lender, but never charged above legal interest. These old citizens did not think it was right to charge over the legal rate for their money. Sixty thousand dollars was about the usual amount that he returned on his tax list. He had a beautiful plantation, well improved, and was a first-class farmer. He had three children, one son George, and two daughters. One of the daughters is the wife of Dr. George Rives. The other was the wife of Thomas Bunting. Mr. Holmes lived to a ripe old age and died on his plantation.

RICHARD W. WALL.

At an early day Richard W. Wall (Uncle Dick, as he was familiarly called) moved from Georgia and settled in this county. He started life with limited means, but soon built up a comfortable estate. He was a very popular man, and was known far and wide for his lively disposition and witicisms and droll sayings. He was always ready for a frolic or foot race, as he called it. He was fond of hunting, fishing, etc., and was always the life of the party. At every Fourth of July barbecue, or political gathering, he would take an active part, and was generally master of ceremonies. In politics he was a Whig, but he was very liberal in his views. He was a privileged character in his own county, and did and said what he pleased, and his jokes and frolics were always taken, as a matter of course, but on one occasion Uncle Dick went to Greenville, Butler county, on a visit to a married daughter, where he was also very popular.

Circuit Court was in session, with Judge Dougherty on the Bench. Uncle Dick had been running with the boys, and was feeling pretty good. The sheriff was standing on the portico of the court-house call- the names of witnesses. Uncle Dick was intimate with him, and said to him, "You Butler county sher- iffs don't know how to call witnesses; let me show you how we do it in Montgomery county." And in full view of the Judge, who was sitting on the stand and looking on, he cried at the very top of his voice, "Peter Plunket, Peter Plunket, come into court you red headed rascal." The Judge, doing his best to repress a smile, said "Mr. sheriff, take the gentleman around to the jail, for contempt of court." His friends, however, came to his rescue and begged him off, and got the Judge to change the sentence to a small fine; and uncle Dick never heard the last of Peter Plunket, but he took the joke very pleasantly.

Mr. Wall was a whole-souled, genial, good. man. His wife was a good christian lady, and they raised a large family of sons and daughters. Late in life Mr. Wall sold out and moved to Texas, where he spent the remainder of his days, and at a ripe old age died loved and respected by the new friends that he had made, and his old friends at home.

WILLIAM TAYLOR.

Brick House Billy Taylor was another of the early settlers. He was very wealthy and owned the land along the Norman Bridge road, known now as the

Carr, Mason, Walters Brothers, Mrs. W. T. Taylor, Leigh, Armistead and J. R. Adams places. Mr. Taylor was a great business man, and correct in all his dealings with his fellow men. His wife was a daughter of Abner McGehee, as has been mentioned in a former chapter. They raised a large family of children. Mr. Taylor spent the declining years of his life in the city, where he died at an advanced age.

PETER B. MASTIN.

Peter B. Mastin was one of the earliest settlers on Ramer creek. He came to the county about the year 1834. In 1836 he married Mary Myrick and started in life. They had only a limited property at first, but Mr. Mastin was a man of energy and enterprise. He was a good farmer and made his business pay, and they soon built up an estate. Mr. Mastin was the second man who built a mill on Ramer creek. He ground the corn for the surrounding country for a number of years. He had also attached to his mill an old-fashioned upright saw, and made quantities of lumber which he could always sell. Daniel Malloy had a plantation below Mastin's mill which was subject to overflow, and Mr. Malloy came to the conclusion that Mastin's mill-dam was the cause of it, and he brought suit against Mastin to recover damages. At the trial Warren Williams, an honest, uneducated fellow, was a witness, and while on the stand was asked if Mastin's mill was removed could Malloy control the water? "Oh yes," said Mr. Williams, "it could be controlled." Every one was eager to hear how it could be done. "Please state how it could be done." He said, "Commence above Malloy's land and dig a canal broad and deep enough to hold the water, right under Malloy's land, and run it out right below Malloy's land, and then you have got it." Malloy lost his case.

Mr. Mastin remained on his plantation a number of years, and then bought a plantation near the city, built a fine residence and removed his family to it, where he lived the remainder of his life. He died at not an advanced age. Mr. Mastin was the father of Mrs. Hamilton McIntyre and of Thomas and Peter B. Mastin.

VINCENT R. PORTER.

Vincent R. Porter moved from Georgia when a young man and engaged with Dr. S. C. Oliver on his plantation. He shortly afterwards married Sarah McGehee, niece of Abner McGehee. They commenced life with moderate means, but soon bought a plantation and built up a comfortable home. Mr. Porter was one of the best farmers of his day, and was looked upon as a level headed, practical man. He was a good citizen and neighbor and a correct, upright man. He lived to the age of eighty-six years and died at the original old home. His widow is still living. They reared a large family of children.

WILLIAM D. SANKEY.

About the year 1830 William D. Sankey moved from Talliferro county, Georgia, to Montgomery county and settled in the prairies about fifteen miles south of the city. Mr. Sankey was a man who was respected for his many good qualities; he was a moral sober man who exerted a good influence in the community in which he lived. He was noted for his generosity and liberality, and was a supporter of the Presbyterian church and believed in the doctrine of the same. His wife was Margarette Daniel, and they had four children born to them. The oldest son, Dr. John F., married a daughter of James Daniel. Richard, another son, married a Miss Watts. Bettie, a daughter, married Edward Leonard, a popular and promising young man. Laura, the oldest daughter, never married. Mr. Sankey lived to a good old age and died at the old homestead.

JAMES C. SANKEY.

James C. Sankey was a brother of W. D. Sankey, and was considered a rich young bachelor when he first came to Montgomery county. In the year 1836 he volunteered and went to Florida to fight the Indians. Oceola was the chief; a bold, dare-devil of an Indian who declared war against the United States. In a fight in the Florida glades young Sankey received a wound. He was the only man

in his company who was wounded, and when he
came home he brought with him a Seminole bullet.
This gave him considerable prominence and made
him very popular. At that time the militia of the
county was well organized; every man of proper
age had to do militia duty or pay a fine. Sankey
was elected Colonel of the Regiment without any
solicitation on his part. He was a very modest and
unassuming man, but accepted the commission and
discharged its duties with credit to himself. He
afterwards married Frances Ruddle, an adopted
daughter of James Daniel. Col. Sankey was a member of the Presbyterian church, and regarded by all
who knew him as a devout christian, kind neighbor
and good citizen. He died at a ripe old age, and
left besides his property and children a good name.

JAMES DANIEL.

James Daniel was another of those good old
settlers. His plantation joined the plantation of W.
D. Sankey. Mr. Daniel was a plain, unassuming,

good old man, loved and respected by his neighbors and friends. He was correct in all his dealings with his fellow men. He loved his home, family and friends, and at an advanced age died without an enemy.

JOSEPH FOSTER.

Joseph Foster was another early settler from Georgia. He settled in the Sankey neighborhood, and was in very comfortable circumstances. He established a plow and wagon factory in connection with his farm, and for a long number of years supplied the surrounding country with wagons and plows. There were no wagons shipped at that early day, and Mr. Foster's wagons were in great demand. He was a very useful man in his vicinity, correct in all his dealings with his fellow men, and a leading member of the Baptist church. His wife was a Miss Daniel, and sister of Mrs. W. D. Sankey. They had a large family of children—three sons and six daughters.

7

William, his oldest son, was a Professor, and taught school a number of years in the city. Two of the daughters married John H. and Thomas Robertson (brothers), another married James Collins, another married William Wilkerson, and another married Prof. Barton.

Mr. Foster lived to a very old age, and died at the old homestead. The family are all dead except one son, James Foster of Huntsville, and Mrs. Wilkerson of Ft. Deposit.

WADE H. ALLEN.

Wade H. Allen was another of these old settlers, and was a man of extraordinary energy and enter-prise. He was possessed of sound practical sense and succeeded in everything that he undertook. In addition to his planting interest, he obtained from the government the contract for carrying the mails from Montgomery to Mobile, and established a line of four-horse coaches and carried passengers to and from Mobile. He held the contract until the Montgomery and Pensacola Railroad was built, and managed the business to the satisfaction of the government and made it profitable to himself. Mr. Allen was a correct man in all his dealings, and was an influential man in his day. His first wife was a daughter of Dennis Carpenter; his second wife was Eliza Sayre, daughter of Calvin Sayre, a New Jersey family. He was the father, by his second wife, of Gen. W. W. Allen and of Wade H. and George E. Allen. One daughter was the wife of Gov. Thomas H. Watts; another was the wife of Dr. McBride, who after his death married Mr. Theiss. He was the grandfather of Wade H. McBride, Mrs. I. R. Faunce and Mrs. Frank P. O'Brien.

GEORGE POWELL.

George Powell was among the very first of these old settlers. He bought a plantation on the west side of Catoma creek, and engaged in planting. He was known far and wide for his many good qualities of head and heart. He was a Methodist, and helped to organize and establish one of the first Methodist churches in the county. He was liberal and charitable with his means. His home was the home of the preachers of every denomination. He was given to hospitality, and the string of the latch was on the outside of the door. His wife was a daughter of Judge Peter Williamson, a most excellent woman. They had four children—two sons and two daughters. Michael, the oldest son, married a daughter of Maj. Green Wood. Peter G. married a daughter of William Falconer. Sallie, the oldest daughter, married Nicholas Barnett; and Bettie, the youngest, married William Taylor.

Mr. Powell remained on his plantation until the children all married, and then moved with his wife to Tallassee where he lived a number of years, and late in life moved with his son to Kentucky. His wife died soon afterwards, and in a few years he too died at a ripe old age.

JOSHUA JONES.

Joshua Jones was another of those good men; he settled on the Woodly road west of Catoma creek, and soon built up a comfortable property. He was a very successful farmer, and a good and useful man in his community. He was a member of the Baptist church, and a liberal supporter of the same. His wife was a Miss Elizabeth Jones, but not related to her husband; she was noted for her good christian character and kindness of heart. Their home was the home of the orphan, and the string of the latch was on the outside of the door. They reared a family of nine children, seven sons and two daughters. Mr. Jones lived to a good old age. His wife survived his death only a short time, and followed her husband. Two of the sons are living at the old homestead.

LABAN B. UNDERWOOD.

Laban B. Underwood was the first man who settled on the east side of Ramer creek. It was about the year 1822. He settled on a small farm and began life. His wife was Nancy Giles; they commenced with very limited means, but by energy and good management they soon built up a comfortable home. He was a member of the old Primitive Baptist church in good standing, and was an honest, upright and good man. They reared a family of eleven children who lived to be grown,—seven sons and four daughters. Mr. Underwood lived to a good old age and died during the war. His wife survived him a few years and died at the old homestead. Her remains were laid beside her husband. The youngest son and daughter and two grand sons are living at the old homestead.

AUGUSTUS MIDDLETON.

Augustus Middleton was a very early settler in Montgomery county. He first located near the city and then moved west of Pintlala creek, in southwestern portion of the county. Mr. Middleton was an intelligent and well educated man and a first-class citizen. He had a good home and pretty farm, and was a leading man in his community. His wife was

Eliza Goss. They had an excellent family, one son and four daughters. The son is still living, a credit to his family and an honor to his father. Late in life Mr. Middleton united with the Methodist church. He lived to a good old age and died at the old homestead.

ANDERSON MOSLEY.

Anderson Mosley was among those who first settled west of Pinchony creek. He was an honest and correct man in all his dealings and a prominent man in his vicinity. His wife was the daughter of William McLemore, one of the county's best citizens, as mentioned in a former chapter. He raised a large family and was the father of A. M. and J. J. Mosley, living near the old place.

COL. WILLIAM ARMISTEAD.

Col. William Armstead, originally from Virginia, settled at an early day in one of the western counties of the state, but at a late day moved with his family to Montgomery county. He bought a plantation about ten miles south of the city. Col. Armstead was a considerable acquisition to the vicinity in which he settled. He was wealthy, intelligent, and a very influential man. He had an excellent family, and they were of the highest order of society and respectability. He was the father of Dr. W. B. Armistead. His oldest daughter was the wife of Elmore Fitzpatrick; another was the wife of P. Tucker Sayre; another was the wife of P. H. S. Gayle, and another was the wife of Richard Goldthwaite.

COLONY FROM SOUTH CAROLINA.

At an early day a small colony emigrated from South Carolina to Montgomery county. They were all prominent men in their day and generation. Their names were, Jesse P. Taylor, Dr. James H. Taylor, Edward Taylor, William Henry Taylor, Dr. C. Bellinger and George W. Hails.

JESSE P. TAYLOR,

Jesse P. Taylor was the richest man among them. His wealth, like all those old citizens, consisted of lands, negroes and money. He owned a large body of prairie land eight or ten miles south of the city. Mr. Taylor had one daughter who married a young lawyer from Georgia by the name of Harwell, and by this marriage one child was born, a daughter. Mr. Taylor settled his son-in-law on a valuable plantation, but in a short time a separation took place. Mrs. Harwell, by her next friend, petitioned to the legislature to have the names of herself and child changed back to Taylor, and ever afterwards she went by the name of Miss Mary Ann Taylor. The child grew to womanhood and married Dr. James, a son of Lorenzo James.

WILLIAM HENRY TAYLOR.

William Henry Taylor and family stood at the head of society. Mr. Taylor was possessed of every quality that it takes to constitute a moral, christian

gentleman.   He was a leading member of the Methodist church and a strong supporter of the same.   Mr.
Taylor at one time was very wealthy, but about the
year 1849 he engaged in a perfectly legitimate cotton
speculation, in which he lost the larger part of his
fortune.   The loss of his property did not have a
tendency to detract from his moral and religious
life.   He died as he had lived, honored and respected
by all who knew him.   His wife was the sister of
George W. Hails.   They had a large family of children.   The daughters were noted for their beauty
and accomplishments.   One of these daughters became the wife of Albert Elmore; the other the wife
of Col. John W. A. Sanford.

DR. JAMES H. TAYLOR.

Dr. Taylor was a man of property, and a practicing
physician and planter.   He had a splendid family.
One son was sheriff of Montgomery county.   One
daughter married Dr. Merriweather Gilmer; and
another was the wife of Francis M. Gilmer, Jr.

DR. C. BELLINGER.

Dr. Bellinger was a man of the very highest order of moral and christian worth; a man whose very appearance would strike you with admiration and respect. Tall, fine looking, pleasant and agreeable, and a magnificent gentleman. He was rich and charitable with his means. In the early part of his life he was a member of the Methodist church, but late in life he changed his religious belief and joined the Catholic church and was a devout member of the same until he died. He owned a large plantation on the head waters of Catoma creek, and about the center of the plantation he had a mound thrown up and upon that mound he had erected a cross, the first and only one ever seen by the writer in the country. Dr. Bellinger lived to a good old age and passed away. One of his daughters married Bush W. Bell; another married Edward R. Holt. Robert Bellinger, of the city, is the only son living. William, his other son, died recently.

GEORGE W. HAILS.

George W. Hails, another of these old settlers from South Carolina, bought a magnificent plantation and became one of the most successful planters in Montgomery county.   He introduced the first two-horse plough, and took great pleasure and pride in calling the attention of his neighbors and friends to the good work it performed.   Mr. Hails was a good citizen, neighbor and friend.   When he died he left a rich legacy ; besides his property he left a splendid family of sons and daughters.

ELBERT HOLT.

Elbert Holt, another of those good old citizens, settled in the vicinity of Oak Grove.   No man stood higher in the good opinion of his people.   He was rich, liberal and charitable, and was ready at all times and] under all circumstances to contribute a full measure of duty towards advancing the cause of morality, sobriety and christianity.   He died at not a very advanced age, loved and respected by his people.

JASON G. JONES.

Jason Jones settled early in life at Oak Grove, and commenced with limited means. By industry and good management, he soon built up a comfortable home and property. Mr. Jones was a plain, modest and unassuming man, and was considered one of the best farmers of his day. His wife was a Miss Peele. They have several sons living in the county. He spent all the years of his life at the old homestead and died as he had lived, an "honest man."

JAMES A. FORNISS.

James A. Forniss, a gentleman from South Carolina, was another of those early settlers. He bought a plantation on the east side of Pintlala creek, on the old Stage road. He was a highly educated man and taught school in various places, and was very popular as an educator. There are men now living who are indebted in part to Mr. Forniss for their education. He was a man of property, and was highly respected as a citizen. His wife was the daughter of Shockley Adams of South Carolina, and was a most excellent woman. She was loved and respected for her many good acts and deeds, prompted by the head and heart of a good woman. They had seven children—two sons and five daughters. One son died in the army, and the other lost a leg. The oldest living daughter married W. G. Robertson, the next married W. R. Forniss of Marengo county, and the youngest is the wife of J. T. Robertson.

SAMUEL L. ARRINGTON.

Col. Samuel L. Arrington moved with his family from North Carolina to Montgomery county, and bought a plantation in the vicinity of Mount Zion church eighteen miles from the city. He was very popular in his native State, and represented his county in the Legislature on several occasions. He was an honest, correct, pleasant and agreeable gentleman, and no man had more friends than Col. Arrington.

After remaining on his plantation a few years, he bought a plantation near the city, where he removed with his family to the regret of his friends and neighbors. Later in life he moved to the city, where he spent the remainder of his days, and died at a good old age, loved and respected by the people of his county. He had an excellent family of children. Judge Thomas M. Arrington and James N. Arrington, Esq., are sons of Col. Arrington.

HARDY WILKINS.

Hardy Wilkins was among the first of the early settlers on the head waters of Ramer creek. Mr. Wilkins was a moral, sober and most excellent man. After remaining on his plantation a number of years, he built a residence at Ramer, and was the first man to move to that place with his family. That move encouraged others to do likewise, and in a few years they had a nice little town. The town of Ramer is noted for its good schools and churches, good society and clever people. Mr. Wilkins was for a number of years before the War United States deputy marshal under Marshal Godbold. He was a member of the Presbyterian church, and was noted for morality and sobriety. He was heard to say that he did not know the taste of whiskey. Late in life he moved to the city where he remained the remaining years of his life, and at the age of about eighty-six he died, having survived every man mentioned in this little book.

OLD CÆSER.

Cæsar Blackwell was one of the most extraordinary negroes of his day. He was a slave and a full blood African. He joined the church at Old Elam and afterwards began to preach on the surrounding plantations. His preaching attracted the attention of the white people, and the Baptist denomination purchased him from Mr. Blackwell, his master, for whom they paid one thousand dollars. They did not set him free, but appointed James McLemore his guardian, and ordained and licensed him and sent him out to preach. He had no education, but could read a chapter and give out a hymn. He visited the churches in company with the white preachers and occupied the pulpits with them. He was not given a separate charge, but aided and assisted the white preachers in their work. He would always be invited home by some of the members of the different churches, and while he did not eat with them at their tables or sleep in their residences, yet he was always made comfortable and welcome wherever he went. His new relationship did not have a tendency to make him forget his place, and he was always an humble and respectful negro. He lived to a good old age, preaching to the end of life, and when he died he was laid away and a stone erected to his memory.

THE DUEL.

There has been but one duel fought in Montgomery county. About the year 1839 Bush W. Bell and John S. Bailey, two very prominent and popular

8

citizens, had a misunderstanding and hot words were passed. A challenge was given and accepted, the day was appointed and the place selected for the fight. The place selected was about twenty miles from the city, on the road just beyond Line creek. Line creek was then the boundary line between the State and the Indian Nation.   The duel was no secret ; everybody knew that a comtemplated duel was to be fought between Bell and Bailey. They procured each a pair of duelling pistols, the finest made at the time. They were rifled barrels, muzzle loaders and about ten inches long. They both practiced with these pistols for several days before the duel ; and it was said that they could step fifteen paces, turn and cut an inch ribbon in two. They were experts in the use of the pistol. No one thought, if they fought, that either of them would get back home alive. When the day arrived the principals, with their seconds, friends and a physician, were on the ground promptly. The preliminary arrangements were soon made, and the ground stepped off, and the principals took their positions. At the words, "one, two, three, fire," they both fired about the

same time, but neither was hurt. Their friends interfered and tried to stop the fight, but it did no
good. They demanded another round, and the next
resulted as the first, nobody hurt. They demanded
the third round, which resulted the same, and so on
until the sixth round, when their friends interfered
again; but the principals were determined to fight
it out, and demanded the seventh round. This duel
was no sham; their pistols were loaded with powder
and lead every time, and these gentlemen were not
cowards, they were anything else; but they seemed
to be unnerved, and would fire too quick. The result of the seventh round was like the others, nobody
hurt. They demanded the eighth round, in which
Bailey received a very severe wound in the fleshy
part of the hip. When Bailey recovered from the
shock he was not satisfied and demanded the ninth
round, in which Bell received a bad wound in the
thigh. Their friends then interfered and forced them
from the field. It took Bell and Bailey a long time
to recover from their wounds. Bell got out first,
and after the excitement of the duel passed off, he
was elected Sheriff of Montgomery county. Bailey

lived and died a respected citizen. It cannot be said that providence had anything to do with this duel, but it did seem that it was not intended for Bell and Bailey to kill each other.

RELATIONSHIP BETWEEN MASTER AND SLAVE.

As all these old settlers and citizens who have been mentioned in this little book were slave owners, a short sketch of the relationship between master and slave will not be out of place. Slavery was a legal institution; these citizens had nothing to do with making slavery; it was handed down from generation to generation, from father to son. They came into possession of their slaves by bequest, by purchase and by increase. A man had as much right to hold negroes as property as he had to hold a horse as property, and the laws of his state and the Constitution of the United States protected him in that right. The law protected the master, and the law also protected the slave. If a master did not furnish his slaves with a sufficient amount of food and clothing, and humane treatment, it was made a crime, and he was liable to be prosecuted by the Grand Jury of his county. But it was to the interest of the master to take good care of his slaves; it was a property too valuable to be neglected or abused. Each master enacted a code of laws for the management of his slaves, just as a state enacts a code of laws for the government of its citizens. If the slaves violated one of the laws he was liable to be punished, and the punishment was graded by the offense committed. If the offense was light, the punishment was light; if the offense was greater, the punishment was greater. The owner did not take pleasure in punishing his slaves; he only did it to make them obey the law. Take the code of Alabama as a parallel; if a citizen violates a law, he is punished, and his punishment is in proportion to the offense he has committed. The jury trying the case does not take pleasure in finding a defendant guilty, neither does a judge take pleasure in passing sentence on a criminal. They do it to make them obey the law. The slave was contented and satisfied with his lot in life. The generation that had preceded him were slaves, and from birth they were taught by precept and example to look up to, depend upon and obey their masters in all things. It became natural for them to do so, and thus it was from generation to generation. The slave was not only satisfied and contented with his lot in life, but he was a happy being. He had his house and garden, his food and clothing furnished him, and the very best nursing and medical attention given him when sick. He had his associates, and enjoyed life in his way, just as other people do. He worked along cheerfully all day, and would pick the banjo and sing and dance all night if permitted. He had no cares and responsibilities, had nothing to disturb his mind; he was only required to labor, and all men are required to labor, and will be till the end of time. He was a trusty and faithful being. The master could go from home and remain away on business or pleasure as long as necessary, and leave the wife and children surrounded by these slaves, and they would be as safe from harm as if they were in a palace. Not only were they safe, but they would be protected and defended, if need be. There is not an instance on record in Montgomery county, during the existence of slavery, where a wife or daughter was ever assaulted by a slave. Such a thing was never heard of until the negro was made free. There are only two instances where a slave killed his master during the forty-three years of slavery in Montgomery county.

The society where slavery existed was the best in the world. They were, as a rule, moral, religious, benevolent, peaceable, kind and indulgent, and their precept and example had a good effect on these slaves. There were very few violations of law on the part of these slaves, and their conduct was such that the time of the courts was rarely ever taken up with cases against them. Whereas, now the time of the courts is almost altogether occupied in trying offenders for violations of law against their free brothers, as the chain-gangs, jails, coal mines, and the penitentiary will testify.

In the matter of religion and religious privileges, the slaves had all that their masters had. In all the old country churches a portion of the building was set apart for their benefit, and master and slave worshipped under the same roof. They not only had the privilege of going to church, but were encouraged to go; and they could unite with the church and have their names entered on the same book with their masters. The preacher in charge would baptise them with seemingly as much pleasure as he would the master; and likewise when they partook of the sacrament, after the white members had been waited on, the deacons, who were very frequently the masters, would pass the bread and wine around to them.

When the old family servants had grown grey, when they had served their generation, they would be superannuated and moved up nearer the "big house," where they could be better waited on, and have especial attention given them to the end. Over a quarter century has passed since the slave received his freedom, and those who are still living can be recognized by their polite and respectful behavior, steady habits and good working qualities.

GOOD CITIZENSHIP.

MONTGOMERY COUNTY is one of the oldest counties in the State. It had the richest and greatest variety of soil, and it offered every inducement to these old settlers, and they were not slow in taking advantage of their opportunity. They not only reaped the advantage to themselves, but the generations that followed have been benefitted. These old citizens mentioned were a remarkable people. Not one of them were accustomed to use vulgar or profane language, or to get drunk, play cards. carry concealed weapons, or violate the law. In fact the people all over the county were noted for good morals and good citizenship. There have been fewer violations of law, in proportion to the population, than any other county in the State. From the very earliest days up to the beginning of the war, there were not over twenty men killed in Montgomery county. And in every instance where a white man was charged with murder or manslaughter, except in the case of two men mentioned in the first chapter, they were acquitted by a jury of their countrymen. During the same period only two men were ever charged with the offense of rape, and they were both acquitted by a jury. Only two masters were killed by their slaves, to-wit: Dr. McDonald, at Mt. Meigs, and Alfred Jones, on his plantation. Only two men committed suicide—D. Holman, at Sharpsville, and Booker Hudson, who cut his wife's throat and then cut his own and both died together. One man named Armstrong killed a brother, and Dr. Marler killed a brother. About four men were murdered by parties unknown, and the others were cases of man-slaughter.

This covers a period of about forty-two years, and is an average of about one case in every two years. Where can there be found another county with such a record? The question might be asked what produced this happy result. It is easily answered. It was the moral and religious influence of those departed early settlers over their children and neighbors. Train a child in the way he should go, and when he is old he will not depart from it. That good influence is still felt, and the good example is still being followed. From the close of the war up to the present day, the records of the courts, so far as relates to the native white population in Montgomery connty, shows that same obedience and respect for the majesty of the law as was shown by the original old settlers. And no county or State can boast of a more moral, intelligent and respectable citizenship.

WEALTH OF PLANTERS.

Along about this period, and on to the beginning of the war, the principal wealth of the county was in the hands of the planters. This wealth consisted in lands, negroes and money. The merchants and bankers borrowed money from them, and the legal rate of interest, "eight per cent," was all that was charged. In fact, any man of good character and standing, rich or poor, could always borrow money from these planters, and the only paper required was a plain promissory note, bearing the legal rate of interest, without security. There were no mortgages or crop-lien notes in those days. Confidence existed between man and man. Men were expected to be honest, they were expected to comply with their obligations and to pay their debts, and as a rule they did so. These old citizens and settlers lived on their plantations, built comfortable houses, planted out orchards and shade trees, beautified their homes, established the best society in the world, visited their relatives and neighbors, and supported and sustained the old country churches. They were given to charity and hospitality. The sick and the afflicted received their attention and the stranger at the gate was taken in.

THE BAPTIST CHURCH.

The Baptist church at the earliest settlement of the county was the prevailing denomination. They had more churches and larger congregations. This was before the division, when there was only one Baptist denomination. They were quite democratic in their views and customs. They claimed that each church was sovereign and independent. They did not let any one dictate to them or influence them in their mode of worship. They called their own preachers and they did not fix a salary, in fact nothing was ever said about a salary. Each member paid what he could afford, or nothing, as he saw proper. They took the Bible for the man of their council. They claimed that they did not advocate any doctrine or principle not laid down in the Bible. They claimed that they had Bible authority for believing in the doctrine of predestination and the final perseverance of the saints. They believed in the foreknowledge of God, and that God did, before the foundation of the world, ordain that a portion of the world should be saved and a portion be lost. They believed in baptism by immersion and close communion. They contended that the baptism of Christ by John was their authority for baptism; that Christ was baptized by immersion in the river; that they went down in the water and John did baptize him; and they both came up out of the water. They practiced foot washing, and claimed Bible authority for the same; as Christ before his crucifixion called his disciples together and took a basin of water and girded a towel around his loins, and got down and washed his disciples' feet, and wiped them with the towel, and said: "As your Lord and Master have washed your

feet, ye ought, also, to wash oneanother's feet."
They were opposed to all secret societies and organizations, and contended that the Bibile was a sufficient guide to control the actions of all mankind in
whatever capacity. The Baptist church, at the time
we write, claimed that they had descended from a
direct line of succession from the day of John the
Baptist. That it had been handed down from generation to generation, from father to son. Now this
old Baptist family that had worshiped the same God
had been baptized, as it were, at the same baptismal
fount, and had partaken of the emblems of the
broken body and shed blood of their Savior at the
same sacramental board, was about to separate and
dissolve. The question of foreign and domestic missions had been agitating the church for a number of
years, part of the membership being in favor and
part opposing.

At an association held with Bethel church in the
southwestern portion of the county (the old church
building is still standing), on Monday after the first
Sunday in October, 1837, the separation took place.
It was painful and distressing to see this old Baptist

family part company. Sons leaving their fathers
daughters leaving their mothers. (It is supposed
that the writer is the only person now living that
witnessed this separation.) The separation was final
and forever. From that day there were two separate
and distinct Baptist churches, the original old Primitive and the Missionary churches. The Missionary
church, from the day of the separation to the present
day, have added member to member, church to
church, mission to mission, and have spent millions
of money in extending the cause of christianity.
They have followed the Bible injunction: "Go ye
into all the world and preach my gospel." The
original old Primitive family are still in existence;
they still hold to the old faith and practice. It is a
good old family; they are honest, good citizens and
neighbors; straightforward and correct in all their
dealings with their fellowman; drink a dram whenever they want to, but never drink to excess. They
were the original old soldiers of the cross, and served
their day and generation, and have accomplished a
good work.

THE METHODIST CHURCH IN THE EARLY DAYS.

The Methodist church in those early days had only a limited membership, but after the country was laid off in districts and circuits, it increased rapidly in church organizations and membership. They discarded the doctrine of predestination and election. They believed in baptism, either by sprinkling, pouring or immersion, as the applicant desired. They believed in open communion, and extended invitations to all orthodox christians to the sacramental board. They believed in foreign and domestic missions and were in favor of an educated ministry. The government and usages of the church in that day were about the same as at present. On each of the circuits the members and citizens would construct preaching places, sometimes at school houses, private houses, and when the weather was favorable, under bush arbors. The preachers were expected to preach each day in the week, unless providentially hindered, and they would have a congregation every time. The Conference had a method of doing business, and that was why they were called the Methodist church, and it required hard and faithful labor at the hands of its preachers. Those preachers generally arrived at their appointment about the usual hour. They would dismount from their horses (there were no buggies in those days), and walk directly into the church, without speaking to anyone, and begin services. As soon as the service was over, there would be a general hand shaking between the preacher and congregation. When the congregation got ready to leave, some brother or friend living in the direction of his next appointment would take him home, give him the best they had, and be glad of his company. The next morning he would go to his next appointment, and so on all around the circuit once a month all the year round. Each one of these preachers received one hundred dollars, appropriated out of the general fund of the conference, for his incidental expenses. If he had a family they were provided for, but the majority of them were single men. If one of these preachers joined the conference, expecting to have an easy time and to be sent where he wanted to go, he was generally

9

disappointed. He had to go where he was sent, and he was expected to go without complaint. There could have been no earthly motive for those good men to enter the ministry; their only motive was to do their Master's will and preach the gospel to the people. Some of those early circuit riders have made great preachers; they have made elders, doctors and bishops, The Methodist church, since that early day, has grown in grace, knowledge and members. It has added member to member, church to church, mission to mission, and has spent millions in extending the cause of christianity all over the world, and the good work is still going on. This generation of preachers have passed away. Their work was hard; they assisted in organizing and establishing the first churches, and made the work comparatively light for those that were to follow.

REVIEW OF THE OLD CHURCHES IN THE COUNTY.

The first Baptist church organized was in the Fork. William Adkins and Lemuel Fields were among the first members. The next was Antioch, near Mt.

Meigs. Green Pinkston, John and Isaac Ray were among the first members. The next was Elam. William McLemore and a man named Breedlove were among the first members. The next was Bethel, on Pintlala creek. The next was Bethlehem, in the southwestern portion of the county, and the organization is still in existence. The next was Liberty, at Carters Hill. The next was Mt. Pleasant. Laban Underwood, Mr. Evan, Bright Surles, Hardy Robins, and Bryant Walters were among the first members.

The first Methodist church in Montgomery county was established in the fork, with Bernard Young preacher in charge. The next was in 1822 at the old Westcott Grave Yard on the Mobile Road, two miles from the city, and was afterwards moved into the city. Prior to the year 1828 there was a Methodist Episcopal church near David Graves, then in Montgomery county, but now in Lowndes. The Graves and Stones were among its members. The next was established at Oak Grove. Joseph and John Green were among the first members. The next was Hopewell, near Robertson's X Roads, with George Powell and Michael Elsberry members. The next was Bethel, in Township 16, Range 20, with the Gilmers, Barnetts, Howards and Mathews as members. The next was Mt. Zion, near the plantation of Peachy Gilmer, and afterwards moved to Mt. Zion Road, with Reuben Emerson and family, James Miller and family, David Campbell and wife as members. The next Tabernacle, with Rev. Johua Starr as preacher, with John Elsby, Mr. Ledbetter, John Bonham, George N. and John Gilmer, members.

PROVIDENCE CHURCH—PRESBYTERIAN.

About the year 1821, William Sharp, better known as Gentleman Billy Sharp, and Zephanial Johns, two men of Irish descent, moved and settled in Montgomery county. They organized and established the first Presbyterian church in the county outside of the city. That church organization has never been dissolved. The first church was located at a place called Sharpsville, on the Hayneville road. The old burial ground still marks the place. The first pastor in charge was the Rev. Cunningham, who assisted in first organizing and establishing the church. At a later period, and when the old building was about to decay, a new and fine church was built a few miles east on the same road. This was for a long time the finest church building in the county outside the city. The building is still standing, and services are regularly held with a respectable membership and congregation. The pastors of this old church, as well as can be remembered, were the Revs. Cunningham, McNab, Harrison, McKee, Gerdon, Foster, Swift, Sturgeon, Kirkpatrick, White. The Rev. J. C. Sturgeon is now in charge.

MT. MEIGS PRESBYTERIAN CHURCH.

The next and only other Presbyterian church in this county, outside of the city, was established at Mt. Meigs, about the year 1825. This church was established through the influence of that noble christian lady, Mrs. David Talliferro. The membership was small, but composed of the best people. Mrs. Talliferro was the principal supporter of the little church, and she kept it up as long as she lived, but when she died the church died also. The Rev. Fielding Bradshaw was the pastor in charge.

OLD BETHEL CHURCH—BAPTIST.

Old Bethel church is the oldest church organization in Montgomery county. It was organized in
the year 1819, and its organization has never been
dissolved. The first building was of hewn logs.
After a few years, a large frame building was
erected by the influence of George Shackelford and
others, as has been mentioned in a former chapter.
It was at this church that the separation of the Baptist denomination took place, and the old building is
still standing. It had at one time a very large
membership and congregation. The people would
come from a great distance in wagons, carriages,
buggies and ox-carts. The church would frequently
not hold the congregation and they would preach
under the shade of the trees. The membership now
is quite limited, but they meet occasionally and
worship at the old church where their fathers and
grandfathers worshiped in the old days that have
past and gone forever.

CONCLUSION.

Every one of the old settlers and citizens that have been mentioned in this little book are dead. They have gone to their final reward. There was never a blot or stain upon the private or public character of one of them, and no country or climate ever produced a better class of men.

The writer was personally acquainted with every-one of them, and intimately acquainted with most of them, and this little tribute to their memory has been to him a labor of love. As the memory reaches back into the far distant part, and the scenes of boyhood and early manhood days are lived over again; when we remember the old ties, old associations and old surroundings that have past and gone forever; and when we realize that we are still living—and living in the midst of a new generation, new associations, and as it were a new world, the thought occurs, "Why has this been permitted?" and the contemplation of that thought makes the hand that pens this last line tremble and the eyes grow dim.

INDEX.

OLD SETTLERS, SKETCHES OF—

OLD SETTLERS—Continued.

OLD SETTLERS—Continued.

OLD SETTLERS—Continued.

www.ingramcontent.com/pod-product-compliance
Lightning Source LLC
Chambersburg PA
CBHW031127020426
42333CB00012B/262